AMISH Family Table

AMISH Family Table

Traditional Breakfasts, Soups, Casseroles, Breads & Desserts

Sara Daigle

with Mary Lapp and Suzanne Jantzi

Foreword by Linda Byler

Photographs by Bonnie Matthews and Abigail Gehring Lawrence

New York, New York

Recipe photos by Bonnie Matthews. Lifestyle photos (pages vi, viii, ix, 44, 130, 226, 228, and 230) by Abigail Gehring Lawrence.

Good Books books may be purchased in bulk at special discounts for sales promotion, corporate gifts, fund-raising, or educational purposes. Special editions can also be created to specifications. For details, contact the Special Sales Department, Good Books, 307 Fifth Avenue, 4th Floor, New York, NY 10016 or info@skyhorsepublishing.com.

Good Books is an imprint of Skyhorse Publishing, Inc.®, a Delaware corporation.

Visit our website at www.goodbooks.com.

10 9 8 7 6 5 4 3 2 1

Library of Congress Cataloging-in-Publication Data is available on file.

Cover design by Kai Texel
Cover photo by Bonnie Matthews

Print ISBN: 978-1-964219-04-2
Ebook ISBN: 978-1-964219-33-2

Printed in China

CONTENTS

FOREWORD

by Linda Byler

The family table has always held an important place in our heritage. From my Grandmother Weaver comes an amazing array of pies—old-fashioned custard and raisin and pecan—with perfect flaky crusts made with lard rendered from their own butchering. These recipes were handed down through generations of good cooks to my sister Mary and her husband David, who are the parents of Sara Daigle. With ten children around her table, my mother taught cooking skills to her daughters, who carried them to their own homes like a torch passed from one kitchen to the next.

David and Mary lived on a dairy farm, and Mary was a proficient gardener. Her loving care of long rows of fresh organic vegetables were canned or frozen, and turned into delicious casseroles or soups and stews. Asparagus, rhubarb, peas, green beans, and plump ears of corn arrived at their table in season, with Mary's special touch.

There is that certain know-how, the feel of bread dough or pie crust too sticky or too crumbly. A little more shortening or another tablespoon of water, a pinch of salt—it all reflects that uncanny ability to get it "just right."

How grateful we are for this talent to preside over a table of homemade food, handed down through generations of skilled cooks. This cookbook takes those skills and translates them into easy-to-follow recipes so that anyone can share good food with those they love. A true blessing to be seated around a table, the happy faces of children, the lively chatter about their day while their bodies are strengthened by the nourishing food and the love of good parents creating a firm structure, the ties that bind.

Praise God for family tables everywhere.

INTRODUCTION

It came three times a day, that familiar call to gather ten children around the family table. I still remember Dad walking upstairs to wake and carry the toddler downstairs to join the rest of the family for breakfast, and how sleepy faces were kissed and adored before they ate eggs, toast, and oatmeal with the rest of us.

Dad always said—and we agreed—that no family should be without the delights of a two-year-old child.

What we thought was plain and simple was called "king's food" by others. It took later years of being away from the garden and farm food to show me why. Nothing in all the world tastes like Mom's homemade chicken pot pie paired with squash casserole, coleslaw (with cabbage straight out of the garden), and chocolate cake for dessert.

As a small child, one bag of any crunchy snack was a rare treat. We all sat cross-legged around the same bag, hoping our siblings wouldn't eat too much, too fast. We'd urge the others to chew carefully and empty their mouths before taking another corn puff or potato chip. We laugh about it now, but to this day I may or may not be seen with five salty snack bags around me on a camping trip.

I don't know how my parents raised ten children, but they did. Some years we were poor, even to our standards, and meals consisted of soup made from green peas and milk with a dab of butter and a dash of salt. Of course, we grew the peas, had a cow for the milk, and churned our own butter. Salt and pepper were affordable, but saltine crackers were a treat and mostly had to be put in soup rather than snacked on, so they'd last longer.

Dad pushed through all odds to provide for our family, so we have only memories of full stomachs and warm beds, with hearts that were loved unconditionally. In later years, we pulled out of hard times—but regardless, my parents had more than enough food at every meal. We fed everyone who walked through our door, and there were always leftovers.

Our family table was special because others found home there, with us. Everyone, at all times, was welcome to pull up a chair and hold his plate out to the center for Mom to fill with baked chicken, mashed potatoes, and fresh green beans. The meal wasn't over until large slabs of pie were downed before we cleared the table, only to set it again several hours later.

Welcome to the *Amish Family Table*! I hope you feel as warmly welcomed to this book as we did gathering around the wooden table with ten siblings and two committed parents who taught us to appreciate the simple, worship the One, and love all.

AMISH
Family Table

Breads and Breakfast

MOM'S SOURDOUGH BREAD

The best thing about going home to Mom's kitchen is waking up to hot bread ready for breakfast. Mom makes anything look easy, but the bread tastes like a million ingredients were used to create it, rather than just three, which is the miracle of water, flour, and salt.

Makes 2 loaves

Ingredients:

3¾ cups warm water
1 cup active sourdough starter
3 teaspoons salt
7 cups unbleached all-purpose flour, divided

Directions:

1. In plastic or glass bowl, mix water and sourdough starter.
2. Add salt and 4 cups flour and stir well.
3. Add remaining 3 cups flour and mix until all flour is well blended.
4. Allow to set for 30 minutes, then stretch and fold.
5. Let set for 30 minutes more, then stretch and fold again.
6. Repeat one more time, then allow to rise at room temperature for 8–12 hours.
7. Stretch and fold once more, then shape into 2 round loaves.
8. Put into round bowls lined with parchment paper.
9. Allow to rise until doubled in size then bake at 425°F in preheated covered Dutch ovens for 30 minutes.
10. Uncover and bake for 30 more minutes.
11. Remove from oven, slice, and serve warm with butter.

POTATO DINNER ROLLS

My twenty-year-old sister made and froze these extra soft potato rolls ahead of time for her own 350 wedding guests. This was just the beginning of culinary talent carried into her own kitchen with six daughters, all of whom learned how to cook from their mother. I do believe all six of the rest of us girls wish to be her neighbor so we could eat from her kitchen!

Makes 30 rolls

Ingredients:

1 cup lukewarm water
4 cups warm milk
2 cups potatoes, mashed
1 cup butter
1 cup sugar
2 eggs, beaten
1 tablespoon salt
2 packages instant yeast
17 cups all-purpose flour

Directions:

1. Mix ingredients in order given, adding flour last and kneading until dough is soft and pliable. Keep kneading for 10 minutes.
2. Let rise until double, then shape into rolls of your desired size. Place on a baking sheet and let rise until doubled.
3. Bake at 350°F for 20 minutes or until golden brown.

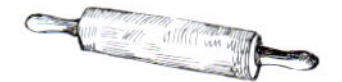

HERB BREAD BRAID

The miracle of yeast is that it turns ordinary flour into something that makes everyone smile. This braid is beautiful and so fun to create! An herbal twist gives it the flair needed to pair perfectly with a bowl of potato soup.

Makes 1 loaf

Ingredients:

1 ½ tablespoons instant yeast
1 cup warm water
¼ cup sugar
1 egg
2 tablespoons vegetable or canola oil
½ teaspoon salt
½ teaspoon Italian seasoning
½ teaspoon parsley flakes
½ teaspoon garlic powder
3 cups all-purpose flour

Directions:

1. Mix in order given, kneading well at the end to ensure a soft and elastic-like dough. If needed, use additional flour.
2. Let rise until doubled.
3. Preheat oven to 350°F.
4. Divide dough into 3 equal amounts, then roll each piece into a rope. Lay side by side, and braid. Tuck the ends underneath.
5. Place braid onto greased baking sheet.
6. Bake for 30 minutes or until golden brown.

PUMPKIN BREAD

In fall, the Amish table is loaded with all things pumpkin, often made with fresh pumpkin from the garden. Pies are a must, but we think the common loaf of pumpkin bread is always a treat.

Makes 2 loaves

Ingredients:

4 eggs, beaten
1 cup canola oil
2 cups white sugar
1 ½ teaspoons salt
1 teaspoon cinnamon
1 teaspoon nutmeg
2 teaspoons baking soda
3 cups all-purpose flour
⅔ cup water
1 cup pureed pumpkin
1 cup walnuts, optional

Directions:

1. Grease 2 loaf pans and preheat oven to 350°F.
2. Beat eggs and add oil, sugar, spices, and baking soda.
3. Stir in flour, alternating with water in small amounts.
4. Gently fold in pumpkin just until mixed. Fold in walnuts, if using.
5. Pour into prepared loaf pans and bake for 30 minutes or until toothpick inserted into center of the loaves comes out clean.

ZUCCHINI BREAD

When gardens are bursting with zucchini, Amish women come up with all kinds of ways to utilize them. When zucchinis grew too fast, we fed the biggest ones to the chickens. Mom loved harvesting them at just the right time, and we loved snacking on the bread she made from them.

Makes 2 loaves

Ingredients:

3 eggs
2 cups sugar
1 cup vegetable oil
1 tablespoon vanilla
2½ cups all-purpose flour
2 teaspoons cinnamon
1 teaspoon salt
1 teaspoon baking soda
2 cups shredded zucchini (no need to peel)
½ cup walnuts, chopped (optional)

Directions:

1. Grease 2 loaf pans and preheat oven to 350°F.
2. Mix eggs, sugar, vegetable oil, and vanilla together thoroughly.
3. Add flour, spices, and baking soda.
4. Add zucchini and mix. Fold in walnuts, if using.
5. Pour into prepared loaf pans and bake for 60 minutes, or until toothpick inserted in center of loaves comes out clean.

MOLLY'S BREAD

Every girl in the family knows the phrase "Molly's Bread"—but whether she was a distant aunt or cousin, I have no idea. Her bread recipe, however, was copied into many a recipe box and made thousands of times in her relatives' kitchens. We think there is nothing in all the world like a hot slice of Molly's bread oozing with homemade butter churned out of fresh cream from the family cow.

Makes 7 loaves

Ingredients:

3½ cups boiling water
2 cups quick oats
2 tablespoons active dry yeast
1½ cups warm water
4 eggs, beaten
1 cup honey
2 tablespoons salt
4 cups whole wheat flour
10 cups all-purpose flour, approximate

Directions:

1. Grease and flour 7 loaf pans.
2. Pour boiling water over oats. Set aside for 30 minutes.
3. Dissolve yeast in warm water, then add yeast mixture to oat mixture.
4. Add eggs, honey, and salt.
5. Stir whole wheat flour into liquid mixture, then keep adding white flour until dough is no longer sticky, kneading as you go.
6. Knead for 10 minutes to create a smooth, elastic dough.
7. Let rise until doubled, punch down, and let rise again.
8. Divide dough into 7 even portions and shape into loaf pans.
9. Let rise until doubled, then bake at 350°F for 30 minutes.
10. Remove from pans, cool, and slice.

BEST CINNAMON ROLLS

I love making these for my children's Christmas breakfast, potluck picnics, gifts, or to add unexpected joy in an ordinary week. Everyone knows mom's kitchen has extra love when these appear out of nowhere!

Makes 20 cinnamon rolls

Ingredients:

Dough:

1 cup cold water
4 cups scalded milk
⅔ cup butter
5 eggs
1 cup sugar
2 teaspoons salt
2 tablespoons instant yeast
12 cups all-purpose flour, approximate

Filling:

½ cup brown sugar
2 tablespoons cinnamon

Frosting:

1 cup butter
1 cup brown sugar
½ cup heavy cream
3½ cups confectioners' sugar

Directions:

1. Mix dough ingredients in order given, slowly adding additional flour if needed, until consistency is soft and elastic-like.
2. Let rise until the dough is doubled in size. Punch down and let rise again.
3. Roll dough with a rolling pin into a rectangle about ½-inch thick.
4. Evenly spread brown sugar on top and sprinkle with cinnamon.
5. Starting with the long side of the rectangle, roll the dough into a log.
6. Slice the log into pieces about 1½ inches thick.
7. Lay pieces in a 9 × 13-inch greased baking pan and let rise until doubled.
8. Bake at 350°F for 20–25 minutes.
9. To make frosting, place butter, brown sugar, and heavy cream in a saucepan and bring to a boil, stirring to dissolve sugar.
10. Remove from heat and add confectioners' sugar. Mix until smooth. Spread on warm rolls.

APPLE DANISH

A glorified Pop Tart, this melt-in-your-mouth pastry makes a golden addition to any hospitality breakfast. It feels more complex than a pie, but is truly easy to create!

Serves 16

Ingredients:

Apple Filling:

6 cups peeled apple slices
1 ⅓ cups sugar
¼ cup butter, melted
2 tablespoons all-purpose flour
1 teaspoon cinnamon

Pastry:

3 cups all-purpose flour
½ teaspoon salt
1 cup butter
1 egg
⅓ cup milk

Glaze:

1 egg white, slightly beaten
½ cup powdered sugar
2 teaspoons water, approximate

Directions:

1. To make the filling, mix all ingredients in order given and set aside.
2. Preheat oven to 350°F.
3. To make the pastry, mix flour and salt, then cut butter into mixture until crumbly.
4. Whisk egg and milk together, then add slowly to flour mixture until you can press dough into a ball. Do not knead.
5. Roll pastry into two oblong shapes large enough to fit on a 10 × 15-inch baking sheet.
6. Line baking sheet with 1 pastry, fill with apple filling, and top with the other pastry.
7. Press edges together firmly and cut slits into top for steam to escape.
8. Bake for 30 minutes or until light brown.
9. Remove from oven and cool.
10. To make the glaze, mix beaten egg white and powdered sugar together, adding just enough water to make a runny glaze to drizzle over danish when it cools. Slice once glaze has set.

RAISED DOUGHNUTS

If you've never tasted Amish doughnut hot out of the oil, you've never really had a doughnut. Krispy Kreme or Dunkin' has nothing on us, we say—and we love serving these to large crowds or to a group of children at a one-room Amish school. Double or triple the recipe for large crowds—make enough to fill a cardboard banana box!

Serves 15

Ingredients:

Doughnuts:

½ cup milk
1½ cups water
4 teaspoons active dry yeast
3¾ cups all-purpose flour, divided
½ cup sugar
2 eggs
½ teaspoon salt
½ cup melted butter
2 quarts vegetable oil, for frying

Glaze:

1½ pounds confectioners' sugar
¾ cup hot water
1 tablespoon butter, melted
1 teaspoon vanilla
1 tablespoon gelatin dissolved in ½ cup cold water.

Directions:

1. Heat milk and water to boiling point and let cool to lukewarm.
2. Add yeast and 2 cups flour. Let mixture rest for 30 minutes, then add sugar, eggs, salt, butter, and the rest of the flour, kneading for ten minutes and adding additional flour if needed to create a soft and pliable dough.
3. Let rise until doubled in size.
4. Roll dough to ½-inch thickness and cut doughnuts.
5. Place cut doughnuts on a well-floured surface and let rise 20 minutes.
6. Pour 2 quarts vegetable oil into an 8-quart pot. Add 2 popcorn kernels. Oil is hot enough to begin frying doughnuts when popcorn kernels pop.
7. Carefully put 3–4 doughnuts in hot oil and fry until golden in color.
8. Flip doughnuts and fry other side.
9. Place on cooling rack or paper towel to absorb extra oil.
10. To make the glaze, mix together the ingredients. Dip both sides of cooled doughnuts in the glaze and place on cooling rack to allow excess glaze to drip.

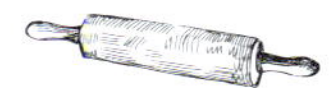

ENERGY BITES

Growing up, I loved making these for my family because they were nutritious, and I always laughed at dad's expression as he bit into a ball of fiber. The beauty of these energy bites is that you can add whatever nuts, seeds, dried fruit, or cereal you like; simply make sure there's enough honey and peanut butter to hold it all together!

Makes 20 energy bites

Ingredients:

3 cups oatmeal
½ cup coconut
½ cup Rice Krispies
½ teaspoon salt
1 ½ cups peanut butter
1 cup honey
1 cup chocolate chips, optional

Directions:

1. Mix ingredients in order given, and shape into walnut-sized balls.
2. Store at room temperature in covered container and grab for easy morning energy!

BREADSTICKS

Yeast is a staple in Amish kitchens, turning humble flour into a vast variety of beautiful golden breads and rolls. These breadsticks are chewy and soft, the perfect accompaniment to a bowl of soup on a cold winter night after barn chores.

Makes 10 large breadsticks

Ingredients:

1 ½ cups warm water
1 tablespoon active dry yeast
4 tablespoons olive oil, divided
1 tablespoon sugar
1 ¼ teaspoons salt
4 cups bread flour
½ cup butter, melted
2 tablespoons parsley flakes
3 tablespoons Parmesan cheese
3 tablespoons garlic powder
Italian salad dressing

Directions:

1. Dissolve yeast in warm water. Add 1 tablespoon oil, sugar, and salt.
2. Mix in flour gradually and knead until dough is smooth and elastic, adding more flour in small amounts if needed to prevent stickiness. Knead for 10 minutes.
3. Set aside and let rise for 20 minutes.
4. Preheat oven to 350°F.
5. Mix 3 tablespoons olive oil, butter, parsley, Parmesan, and garlic powder together, then grease cookie sheet with some of this mixture. Spread dough in pan.
6. Cut dough into strips, then drizzle a little Italian salad dressing and remaining olive oil mixture over breadsticks.
7. Bake for 15 minutes or until lightly browned.

EGG AND COTTAGE CHEESE BAKE

This casserole makes feeding large families a breeze. Prepare the night before, refrigerate, and simply slide into the oven the next morning while coffee brews and the table is set. Pair this with cinnamon rolls, bagels, or toast, and any fresh fruit to equip each family member with enough energy for the day!

Serves 6

Ingredients:

5 eggs
1 (16-ounce) container cottage cheese
1 cup shredded cheddar cheese
¼ cup cooked bacon or ham, chopped
1 (2-ounce) can green chilis
2 tablespoons melted butter
¼ cup all-purpose flour
½ teaspoon baking powder

Directions:

1. Preheat oven to 400°F.
2. Beat eggs, then add all remaining ingredients.
3. Pour into a greased 8 × 11-inch baking dish and bake for 15 minutes. Reduce heat to 350°F and bake for 15 minutes longer or until lightly browned and set.

LAPP FAMILY'S WHOLE WHEAT PANCAKES

Pancakes were a staple at our house, often topped with syrup and fried eggs. Never mind the calories—we needed them all, and gradually learned more about the importance of whole grains. Sometimes we ground our own wheat, but that is not needed to create beautiful brown pancakes!

Serves 8

Ingredients:

2½ cups whole wheat flour
¾ tablespoon baking powder
1 teaspoon salt
1½ teaspoons baking soda
3 eggs, beaten
4½ tablespoons oil
2¼ cups buttermilk
Butter, as needed
Maple syrup, for serving

Directions:

1. Mix dry ingredients together and set aside.
2. In another bowl, mix eggs, oil, and buttermilk.
3. Blend wet mixture into dry and mix well.
4. Heat a cast-iron pan to medium heat, melt ½ teaspoon butter into pan, then pour pancake batter onto butter and fry until bubbles form on top. Flip to other side and fry briefly until center is firm.
5. Serve with fresh butter and real maple syrup.

AUNT SADIE'S WHOLE GRAIN PANCAKES

These pancakes are loaded with nutrition and will give your family a healthy start to their day. Rather than fluffy, they are substantial and grainy, giving a wholesome flavor to every bite. Added wheat bran makes them not just whole grain, but even more fiber-full. We think they're a welcome variation!

Serves 10

Ingredients:

1 cup whole wheat flour
1 cup cornmeal
1 cup oatmeal
1 cup wheat bran
4 teaspoons baking powder
2 eggs, beaten
2 tablespoons oil
Milk to moisten
Butter as needed

Directions:

1. Mix dry ingredients together, then add eggs, oil, and enough milk to create a batter you can pour.
2. Heat a cast-iron pan to medium heat, melt ½ teaspoon butter into pan, then lower heat, pour pancake batter onto butter. Fry on lower heat than most pancakes to give the dense, grainy batter time to fry.
3. When edges begin to set, flip and fry on the other side until center feels firm.
4. You will need to keep adding milk to the batter as the grains soak up liquid the longer they sit.
5. Serve with butter and maple syrup.

AUNT SHERYL'S BAKED OATMEAL

I can't count how many pots of oatmeal we stirred up for the whole family in early morning light, but it was a lot! Mom always made sure we had plenty of brown sugar and fresh milk to pour into our bowls with the cooked oats. But when we started baking this delightful dish, we thought it even better. At our house, oatmeal in all forms was a regular staple.

Serves 8

Ingredients:

1 ¼ cups brown sugar
2 teaspoons salt
4 teaspoons baking powder
2 teaspoons cinnamon
6 cups quick oatmeal
1 cup vegetable or canola oil
4 eggs, beaten
2 cups milk

Directions:

1. Preheat oven to 350°F.
2. Mix dry ingredients, then add oil, eggs, and milk.
3. Stir until well mixed, then pour into greased 9 × 13-inch pan and bake for 40 minutes or until center is set.

Tip: For a variation, layer bottom of pan with berries, apples, or other fruit before pouring batter on top. Bake as usual.

MOM'S GRANOLA

Both chewy and crunchy, this granola beats all! We break it off cooled pans and enjoy it as a snack, in a bowl with milk, or sprinkled over yogurt for a nutritious breakfast. Extra milk from the family cow was often turned into vanilla yogurt—and in this way, my parents fed ten children with less money than many need to feed two!

Makes 16 cups

Ingredients:

11 cups quick oatmeal
6 cups coconut
¾ cup brown sugar
1 teaspoon salt
1½ cups honey
2 cups vegetable or canola oil
2 teaspoons vanilla

Directions:

1. Preheat oven to 275°F.
2. Mix oats, coconut, sugar, and salt in large bowl.
3. Heat honey, oil, and vanilla just until hot, then pour over oat mixture and stir quickly until every morsel is coated with liquid.
4. Spread evenly into 2 (10 × 15-inch) cookie sheets and bake for 20 minutes. Switch pans in oven and bake 20–30 minutes longer, or until granola is golden brown.
5. Remove from oven and let set until cool. Do not stir while it cools! This will help it form chunks to break into a covered container.
6. Store at room temperature and enjoy!

BISCUITS SUPREME

We used these biscuits for a base to pour sausage gravy over, or as a side with butter and jam. They can be dropped easily onto a cookie sheet for a quick breakfast or rolled into special shapes for specific occasions. Mom taught us that it didn't take excessive money to show love through food—and we always felt her love through these biscuits!

Makes 12 biscuits

Ingredients:

2 cups all-purpose flour
½ teaspoon salt
4 teaspoons baking powder
½ teaspoon cream of tarter
2 teaspoons sugar
½ cup lard or butter
⅔ cup milk

Directions:

1. Preheat oven to 350°F.
2. Mix all dry ingredients, cut in lard, and use both hands to create a crumbly mixture.
3. Add milk and stir just until mixed. Do not over mix!
4. Drop by tablespoonful onto ungreased cookie sheet and bake for 20 minutes or until golden brown.
5. Serve with butter, honey, homemade jam, or sausage gravy.

MOM'S BREAKFAST CASSEROLE

This hearty breakfast casserole can be made the night before and stored in the refrigerator for an easy breakfast, especially for guests—of which we had plenty! Simply double the recipe if another family is in the house and serve with fruit and toast or cinnamon rolls.

Serves 10

Ingredients:

4 cups frozen hash browns
1 (16-ounce) package bacon
1 green bell pepper, chopped
1 onion, chopped
3 cups shredded cheddar cheese
1 (16-ounce) container cottage cheese
6 tablespoons melted butter
10 eggs
½ teaspoon salt
¼ teaspoon pepper

Directions:

1. Preheat oven to 350°F.
2. Place hash browns in greased 9 × 13-inch pan.
3. Fry bacon, chop, then set aside. Sauté pepper and onion in bacon grease.
4. Sprinkle sauteed vegetables and chopped bacon over hash browns.
5. Mix both cheeses, butter, eggs, and seasonings, then pour over hash browns and bake for 30 minutes or until center is set.

SUZANNE'S PUMPKIN BRAN MUFFINS

If you're looking for extra fiber, this muffin is it! Subtle pumpkin flavors mesh with whole grain flour to create a moist and soft muffin that tops many. Extra bran gives your body the boost it needs. These store well in the pantry for days!

Makes 24 muffins

Ingredients:

4 eggs
2 cups sugar
1½ cups vegetable or canola oil
2 cups cooked and pureed pumpkin
2¾ cups whole wheat or spelt flour
3 cups wheat bran
1 tablespoon cinnamon
2 teaspoons baking soda
1 teaspoon salt
2 teaspoons baking powder

Directions:

1. Preheat oven to 350°F. Grease or line muffin tins.
2. Beat eggs, then add sugar and other wet ingredients and mix well.
3. Add all remaining ingredients and stir well. Fill each muffin cup roughly two-thirds of the way.
4. Bake for 20 minutes or until center is set.
5. Remove from pan to a baking rack, cool, and store in a covered container at room temperature

WHOLE GRAIN WAFFLES

We all love when delicious and nutritious collide—and these waffles prove it's possible! You'll want to begin the night before with a simple oat soak. Create a waffle buffet by letting your children choose peanut butter, maple syrup, fruit, and whipped cream—or anything else that suits your fancy. My father loved chicken gravy over waffles, but I do think that's a bit unusual!

Makes 6 waffles

Ingredients:

2 cups oats, ground (or use oat flour)
2 cups milk
½ cup butter
2 eggs, separated
1 teaspoon baking powder
½ teaspoon salt
2 tablespoons raw sugar

Directions:

1. Pour oats and milk into a dish, cover, and allow to soak overnight in refrigerator.
2. In the morning, whip ½ cup butter until fluffy, then stir in oat mixture.
3. Beat egg whites until fluffy, then add to oat mixture by gently folding spatula from top to bottom of bowl.
4. Add egg yolks and remaining ingredients, then gently fold just until mixed.
5. Heat a waffle iron to medium heat, spray with cooking spray or brush with butter, and pour batter to fill to about ½ inch from the edges before closing lid.
6. Cook until waffle is brown and firm. Remove from waffle iron.
7. Serve immediately with toppings of choice.

EGG DUTCH

Mom often made these for a quick Sunday evening meal. We loved them and didn't need any topping other than ketchup. We always raised chickens on the farm, so we had plenty of fresh brown eggs to turn into nutritious meals. Whatever topping your family loves, these are an easy, but fun, dinner for your family!

Serves 6

Ingredients:

5 eggs
1 teaspoon salt
¼ teaspoon pepper
1 heaping tablespoon all-purpose flour
1 cup milk
Butter

Directions:

1. Beat eggs well, then add all other ingredients except butter and mix well.
2. Melt a small amount of butter in a cast-iron pan over medium heat, then pour ½ cup batter into pan.
3. Fry until set, then flip and fry for a few seconds more.
4. Flip onto a plate and cover with ketchup or whatever topping your family desires.

Soup and Salad

CHEESEBURGER SOUP

This soup is a colorful variation of the usual potato soup we ate a lot. Hamburger and cheese blend beautifully with a creamy white base and colorful vegetables. Pair with fresh bread and butter.

Serves 12

Ingredients:

2 pounds ground beef
6 carrots, chopped
6 potatoes, chopped
3 celery stalks, chopped
1 onion, chopped
¾ cup butter
1 cup all-purpose flour
2 quarts chicken broth
¾ teaspoon pepper
2 teaspoons salt
½ tablespoon chicken base, or 2 cubes chicken bouillon
1 cup shredded cheddar cheese
1 cup milk
¼ cup sour cream

Directions:

1. Sauté ground beef and onions until brown, using a spatula to break up the beef into small pieces as you cook it. Set aside.
2. Add water and other vegetables to a large saucepan, cook until vegetables are soft, then add to ground beef mixture.
3. Melt butter in large soup pot or Dutch oven, then slowly stir in flour to make a thick paste. Slowly add chicken broth, stirring swiftly to avoid lumpiness. Bring to a boil as you stir, until broth is thick and creamy.
4. Add seasonings, cheese, milk, and sour cream to broth mixture and stir until smooth.
5. Pour ground beef and vegetables into milk mixture, stir, and serve.

MOM'S CHILI SOUP

For a more economical chili, we created this soup. We loved it on cold winter nights with hot slabs of thick cornbread and home-churned butter. Nothing more was needed—sometimes the best things in life are the down-home basics enjoyed with family and love in a warm house. Contentment is found when the heart—and stomach—is full.

Serves 12

Ingredients:

2 pounds ground beef
1 large onion, chopped
1 large green pepper, chopped
2 (15-ounce) cans chili beans
2 (15-ounce) cans kidney beans
2 quarts tomato juice
2 cups water
2 teaspoons oregano
1 teaspoon basil
1 tablespoon chili powder
2 tablespoons brown sugar

Directions:

1. In an 8-quart pot, sauté beef, onion, and green pepper until beef is brown.
2. Add remaining ingredients. Simmer 1 hour.

MOM'S WHITE CHICKEN CHILI

Soup is an economical and nutritious way of feeding a large family. We made various kinds often and found guests as appreciative over it as we were. Hospitality wasn't fancy at our table; we simply invited others to belong. I still believe that people don't need to be impressed as much as they need the blessing of gathering and the love of belonging. A hearty pot of soup helps to do just that!

Serves 10

Ingredients:

1 pound chicken breast, cubed
1 onion, chopped
1 tablespoon olive oil
4 (15-ounce) cans great northern beans, rinsed and drained
14.5 ounces (about 2 cups) chicken broth
4 ounces chopped green chilies
1 teaspoon cumin
½ teaspoon black pepper
1 teaspoon oregano
½ tablespoon garlic powder
½ tablespoon chicken base, or two cubes chicken bouillon
2 cups milk
20 ounces sour cream
1 cup half-and-half
1½ cups shredded mozzarella
½ cup shredded cheddar cheese

Directions:

1. Sauté chicken and onion in the oil until chicken is cooked through.
2. Add beans, broth, chilies, and seasoning and simmer for 30 minutes.
3. Add milk, sour cream, half-and-half, and cheeses and heat slowly until cheese is melted.

CREAMY POTATO SOUP

With extra milk from the family cow and potatoes from the garden, this thick, creamy soup was a favorite family staple. White sauce covers each potato cube, and a creamy liquid fills each spoonful for an economical bowl that tastes like it could be found on an expensive restaurant table. Serve with sourdough bread or fresh dinner rolls.

Serves 12

Ingredients:

5 cups diced potatoes
¾ cup diced celery
2 teaspoons salt, divided
½ cup butter
½ cup all-purpose flour
5 cups milk
1 cup heavy cream
½ teaspoon black pepper
½ teaspoon garlic powder
3 hard-boiled eggs, chopped
Fresh parsley, for garnish

Directions:

1. In a 4-quart kettle, boil potatoes and celery with 1 teaspoon salt.
2. In separate saucepan, melt butter, then slowly stir in flour until smooth.
3. Slowly pour in milk and cream, stirring constantly, then add remaining salt and spices.
4. Simmer, stirring constantly with wire whisk, until thick and bubbly.
5. Pour white sauce over soft vegetables and stir gently.
6. Add boiled eggs, stir, and garnish with chopped parsley.

AMISH TOMATO SOUP

There's nothing cozier than tomato soup and grilled cheese on a Sunday evening! Growing up, fresh tomatoes were always plentiful and ready to be turned into soups, sometimes barely escaping rot as the vines loaded heavily enough to fill a wheelbarrow time and again. Mom's homemade bread made the absolute best grilled cheese, which is a perfect accompaniment to this soup.

Serves 12

Ingredients:

1 tablespoon olive oil
1 onion, chopped
8–10 tomatoes, diced
3 cloves garlic, peeled and minced
2 cups water
2 cups milk
1 teaspoon sugar
1 teaspoon dried basil
½ teaspoon dried thyme
Salt and pepper to taste
Fresh basil leaves for garnish

Directions:

1. In a large kettle, heat oil and add chopped onion. Sauté until soft.
2. Add tomatoes and garlic and cook for 1 minute.
3. Add all other ingredients and simmer for 30 minutes.

LAPP FAMILY'S SAUSAGE SOUP

As one of the oldest in a family of ten children, I was often the one to stand and ladle this soup into twelve bowls around the family table. Spicy tomato and sausage pairs well with vegetables and is an excellent way to get vitamins into your children in winter. Served with large slabs of cornbread doused with butter, every person around your table will be warm and happy!

Serves 12

Ingredients:

1 tablespoon oil
1 pound smoked kielbasa, sliced thinly
1 onion, chopped
3 cups water
2 teaspoons chicken soup base
1 teaspoon salt
¼ teaspoon pepper
½ teaspoon thyme
2 bay leaves
3 large carrots, sliced
3 celery stalks, sliced
¼ head cabbage, chopped
2 tablespoons rice
1 (15-ounce) can kidney beans
1 (8-ounce) can tomatoes

Directions:

1. In a large stock pot, fry kielbasa and onion in oil.
2. Add all remaining ingredients, then simmer slowly for 1½ hours.

CHICKEN CORN NOODLE SOUP

Made with our own chickens and corn from the garden, Mom's chicken noodle soup was a meal in itself. In later years, when we realized soup could be purchased in a tin can, we didn't think it tasted like soup at all! We think this chicken soup is a necessary staple in your kitchen, and one your children will appreciate, especially when sickness hits during those winter months.

Serves 20

Ingredients:

5 quarts water
4 chicken breasts or 4–6 chicken legs
1 (12-ounce) package homestyle noodles
1 cup celery, chopped
4 cups frozen corn
1 cup onion, chopped
1 teaspoon celery salt
1 teaspoon onion salt
Salt and pepper to taste
¼ cup chicken soup base
1 tablespoon dried parsley

Directions:

1. In large stock pot, add 5 quarts water to chicken. Boil until tender, then remove chicken and set aside.
2. Strain broth and return to pot.
3. Add all other ingredients and simmer until vegetables are soft and noodles are cooked.
4. Lastly, remove chicken to a cutting board, use two forks to shred the meat, and return the shredded chicken to the soup.

SEVEN-LAYER SALAD

Our usual salads consisted of fresh, chopped lettuce from the garden, but we loved this layered dish for special occasions. Use a glass bowl and enjoy the colors along with the vegetables!

Serves 15

Ingredients:

1 head iceberg lettuce, large
½ red pepper, chopped
½ yellow pepper, chopped
2 cups frozen peas, thawed
4 tomatoes, chopped
5–6 hard-boiled eggs, chopped
2 cups mayo (spread to completely cover the salad)
2–3 cups shredded cheddar cheese
½ cup bacon bits
¼ cup green onion, chopped

Directions:

1. Layer ingredients in large glass bowl, in order given.
2. Cover and refrigerate. If desired, this can be made a day in advance to make guest preparation easier.

FRUIT SALAD

Long rows of strawberries were a regular spring treat at our house. Hours of weeding and harvesting resulted in mom's fruit salad or fresh strawberry pie. But my best memory as a five-year-old girl was finding the biggest and brightest berry to surprise dad with as he worked in the barn.

Serves 20

Ingredients:

½ cup sugar
2 tablespoons cornstarch
¾ cup pineapple juice
⅓ cup orange juice
1 tablespoon lemon juice
10 cups fresh fruit, chopped

Directions:

1. Mix sugar and cornstarch in saucepan.
2. Add juices and bring to a boil, stirring constantly until thick and smooth.
3. Remove from heat and cool, then pour over fresh fruit of your choice.

DANDELION SALAD

Being sent to the meadow to navigate piles of cow poo in search of dandelion greens was a normal part of my childhood. Whether for salad or gravy, Mom needed lots of these greens for her large family, as they shrink quickly when cooked. But what better way for a child to learn how to harvest food grown in the wild, with no human effort except to gather and cook.

Serves 4

Ingredients:

4 slices bacon
2 teaspoons sugar
2 teaspoons vinegar
2 teaspoons all-purpose flour
¾ cup sour cream
Salt and pepper, to taste
1 quart dandelion greens, fresh
2 eggs, hard-boiled and chopped

Directions:

1. Fry bacon and cut into bits. Set aside.
2. Keep 2 tablespoons bacon grease and discard the rest. Add sugar, vinegar, and flour to grease and stir, simmering until thick.
3. Add sour cream, salt, and pepper.
4. Pour over greens while still warm, then add chopped eggs.
5. Serve immediately.

COLESLAW

Fresh cabbage heads in an Amish garden taste more like crunchy candy than a vegetable. We loved chewing on slices of this while we turned it into slaw, and even the core was enjoyed with its turnip-like texture. Coleslaw is an inexpensive vegetable dish served in Amish gatherings and at the family table year-round because of the cabbage's ability to store in cold basements during winter months.

Serves 8

Ingredients:

4½ cups shredded cabbage
½ teaspoon salt
Black pepper
½ cup mayonnaise
1 tablespoon sugar
2 tablespoons chopped onion

Directions:

1. Mix cabbage and salt an hour before you eat. Set aside.
2. Mix rest of ingredients and pour over cabbage, then stir well and serve.

SPRING LETTUCE SALAD

Mom toiled lovingly in the spring dirt as soon as it warmed enough to hold lettuce seeds. Watching the first heads form was fun, and before long the garden had far too much lettuce for one family to eat. We loved making lettuce sandwiches. You'd be surprised how delicious fresh greens are, sandwiched in between thick slices of fresh bread. And no need to spare the mayonnaise—Amish children need all the calories they can get!

Serves 4

Ingredients:

4 cups mixed salad greens
2 hard-boiled eggs, sliced
1 or 2 green onions, chopped

Dressing:

1 cup mayo
1 ½ tablespoons sugar
1 tablespoon white vinegar
¼ cup milk

Directions:

1. Toss together salad greens, eggs, and green onions.
2. Mix Dressing ingredients well and drizzle over salad. Serve immediately.

AUNT SUSIE'S FRUIT SALAD DRESSING

My people are known for adding sugar and butter to most everything! This recipe is no exception. We loved the fruity crème that marinates together to create fresh bursts of flavor in this recipe, especially when Mom used apples and pears in fall!

Serves 10

Ingredients:

2 eggs
1 cup sugar
1 cup pineapple juice
1 tablespoon all-purpose flour
1 ½ tablespoons butter, melted
1 cup whipping cream
10 cups apples, pears, or any kind of fruit you desire
Handful walnuts or pecans, chopped, *optional*

Directions:

1. Beat eggs, then add all other ingredients except whipping cream and fruit and pour into a kettle.
2. Boil slowly over medium heat, stirring constantly. Cook until sauce is thick and creamy.
3. Remove from heat and cool.
4. Whip cream until thick, then add to cooled sauce. Pour sauce over fresh fruit.
5. If desired, add a small handful of chopped walnuts or pecans.

SUZANNE'S POTATO SALAD

This recipe feeds a crowd! For a smaller amount, simply reduce all ingredients by half and enjoy with burgers or at any summer outdoor meal. We love the touch of mustard in a smooth white dressing over soft potato cubes and we hope you do, too!

Serves 30

Ingredients:

12 cups potatoes, cooked and cubed
12 hard-boiled eggs, chopped
2 cups celery, chopped
1 onion, chopped
3 cups mayonnaise
2 tablespoons mustard
1¾ cups sugar
¼ cup vinegar
1 teaspoon salt

Directions:

1. Allow cooked and cubed potatoes to cool and place in large bowl.
2. Add eggs, celery, and onion.
3. Combine all remaining ingredients in a smaller bowl and mix well, then pour over potato mixture and stir until well blended.
4. Store in refrigerator until serving. Best if made the day prior to serving!

BAKED CHICKEN SALAD

Not your usual cold chicken salad, this savory dish is served hot out of the oven. Chicken and rice bring a unique flare to hard-boiled eggs and celery, and the result is absolutely delicious!

Serves 6–8

Ingredients:

2 cups diced cooked chicken
2 cups rice, cooked
1 cup celery, chopped
½ cup almonds, slivered
3 teaspoons onion, grated
2 teaspoons lemon juice
3 eggs, hard-boiled and diced
¾ cup mayonnaise
1 (10.5-ounce) can cream of chicken soup
1 teaspoon salt
½ teaspoon pepper
Potato chips

Directions:

1. Preheat oven to 400°F.
2. Combine all ingredients except potato chips.
3. Place in shallow 9 × 13 baking dish. Top with crushed chips and bake for 30 minutes or until heated through.

Classic Mains and Sides

MOM'S CHICKEN POT PIE

This flaky crust filled with white sauce and chicken couldn't be better. Even as adults, we recently requested these pies at our family reunion and Mom showed up with her arms loaded with chicken pot pie. Together we remembered those days around the long wooden table, devouring this tasty chicken dish.

Serves 12

Ingredients:

2 top and bottom piecrusts (page 185)

Filling:

1 ½ pounds raw chicken breast, cubed
3 tablespoons oil
2 teaspoons salt, divided
½ teaspoon pepper
5 cups chicken broth, divided
1 ½ cups celery, chopped
2 cups carrots, chopped
2 cups potatoes, cubed
1 onion, chopped
1 (12-ounce) package frozen peas
2 cups water

White Sauce:

½ cup butter
½ cup all-purpose flour
1 teaspoon salt
½ teaspoon pepper
1 teaspoon paprika
1 cup heavy cream

Directions:

1. Line 2 pie plates with bottom piecrusts.
2. Sauté chicken in oil, then season with 1 teaspoon salt and pepper. Add 2½ cups chicken broth and simmer 10 minutes or until chicken is tender.
3. Boil vegetables (except peas) in 2 cups water until tender. Add remaining teaspoon salt. Drain and set aside.
4. Combine chicken, cooked vegetables, and frozen peas.
5. Heat oven to 350°F.
6. For white sauce, melt butter in saucepan. Stir in flour and seasonings with a wire whisk, then slowly add remaining 2½ cups chicken broth and heavy cream. Stir constantly until boiling, then reduce heat and simmer until thick.
7. Remove from heat and pour over chicken mixture.
8. Divide chicken mixture evenly into 2 unbaked piecrusts, then cover with top crusts.
9. Bake for 40 minutes or until top crusts are golden brown.

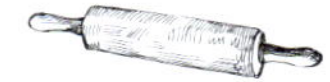

SAVORY BEEF STEW

Processing beef on the farm was a day to remember, but the end result was large, juicy chunks of fresh meat to can for stew days in winter. This recipe is easy and nutritious, a nourishing comfort food and tasty variation from soup. Serve with fresh, warm bread and enjoy!

Serves 12

Ingredients:

2 pounds beef, cubed
¼ cup olive oil
3 tablespoons instant tapioca
10 ounces beef broth or 2½ cups water with 1 tablespoon beef bouillon
⅛ teaspoon garlic powder
1 tablespoon parsley flakes
2½ teaspoons salt
¼ teaspoon pepper
1 (15-ounce) can tomatoes
1 large onion, chopped
6 carrots, chopped
3 potatoes, medium sized and cubed
2 celery stalks, diced

Directions:

1. In a large pot, brown beef cubes in oil over medium heat.
2. Add all ingredients except vegetables and bring to a boil.
3. Transfer to a large baking dish and bake at 350°F for 1½ hours or until meat is tender.
4. Add tomatoes and other vegetables and bake for 1 hour longer, or until vegetables are tender.

AMISH CHICKEN SPAGHETTI

This recipe is a creamy departure from your usual spaghetti with tomato sauce. It's a great way to use leftover diced chicken or turkey! Garlic bread is a delicious addition to this white pasta dish.

Serves 10

Ingredients:

1 (16-ounce) box spaghetti
1 (10.5-ounce) can condensed cream of mushroom soup
1 (10.5-ounce) can cream of chicken soup
8 ounces Velveeta cheese, cubed
½ cup milk
1 teaspoon garlic salt
¼ teaspoon pepper
2 cups cooked chicken bits
¼ cup shredded Parmesan
Fresh parsley to garnish

Directions:

1. Cook spaghetti for 8 minutes, drain, and set aside.
2. In large saucepan, combine soups, Velveeta, milk, and seasonings.
3. Cook over medium heat, stirring constantly until mixture is smooth and cheese is melted.
4. Pour over chicken and cooked spaghetti noodles, toss well, pour into casserole dish, and garnish with parsley.
5. Serve immediately.

MEAT LOAF

For twelve people, it took a lot of ground beef to make meatloaf, so this dish was extra special and remains one of my favorites to this day! Top with ketchup before baking for extra flavor.

Serves 6–8

Ingredients:

2 pounds ground beef
¾ cup dry breadcrumbs
1 cup milk
1 egg, beaten
1 onion, chopped
¼ teaspoon pepper
1¼ teaspoons salt
1 tablespoon Worcestershire sauce
Ketchup

Directions:

1. Preheat oven to 350°F. Grease a 9 × 13-inch baking dish.
2. Combine all ingredients except ketchup in large bowl and mix thoroughly.
3. Pour into baking dish, squirt ketchup on top in a crisscross pattern, and bake for 1½ hours, or until middle no longer shows pink.

SCALLOPED POTATOES

This dish is creamy, savory, and deliciously saucy. We used a handheld shredder for this guest-worthy potato dish, but you could use a food processor if you have one. Serve with any meat of your choice!

Serves 6

Ingredients:

7 potatoes, medium
½ cup onion, chopped
3½ tablespoons all-purpose flour
⅓ cup butter
2½ cups milk
1 teaspoon salt
¼ teaspoon pepper

Directions:

1. Shred potatoes, combine with onions, and place in 2-quart casserole dish.
2. Heat oven to 350°F.
3. Melt butter in saucepan, then slowly stir in flour.
4. With whisk, add milk slowly and simmer until thick and smooth.
5. Add salt and pepper to sauce, then pour over potatoes and mix.
6. Bake for 30 minutes, covered. Uncover and bake 60 minutes longer until potatoes are soft and casserole is browned and bubbly.

BUTTERNUT SQUASH

Spicy kielbasa makes this squash casserole pop! We absolutely love this dish served with fresh bread, salad, and anything else that finds its way onto the family table. Butternut squash are not easy to cut open, but take heart—the effort pays off!

Serves 8

Ingredients:

2 butternut squash, medium-sized
½ cup butter
½ cup half-and-half or heavy cream
Salt and pepper to taste
2 (12-ounce) packages kielbasa

Directions:

1. Preheat oven to 350°F.
2. Cut squash in half, remove seeds, and place halves cut-side down in large baking pan.
3. Add half an inch of water and bake for 45–60 minutes, or until soft.
4. Remove from oven (but leave oven on), cool slightly, then scoop squash out of the shell.
5. Place into large bowl and add butter, half-and-half or cream, salt, and pepper. Mash with potato masher or hand mixer.
6. Slice kielbasa and stir into mashed squash.
7. Put squash into 3-quart casserole dish and bake at 350°F for 30 minutes or until heated through.

SLOPPY JOES

As a child, I remember realizing that everything in my world was different than what I saw outside our Amish community, including Sloppy Joes made with canned beef rather than freshly ground beef. But either way, this dish always made a happy table! You'll want to use fresh or frozen ground beef to replicate this Amish classic.

Serves 8

Ingredients:

1 ½ pounds ground beef
1 small onion, chopped
1 tablespoon brown sugar
¾ teaspoon salt
2 tablespoons mustard
1 tablespoon Worcestershire sauce
½ cup ketchup
½ cup water
Buns or bread

Directions:

1. Brown ground beef with onion, then add all the rest of the ingredients and stir until mixed.
2. Simmer slowly for 5 minutes, stirring occasionally.
3. Serve with your choice of buns or bread.

BAKED CORN

I will always remember the sweet flavor of corn on the cob drenched in butter and sprinkled with salt. From pulling ears of corn off long rows in the garden to serving platters of steaming hot cobs to a long table full of people, there wasn't much left over—but any leftovers could be sliced off the cob and turned into this savory casserole the next day.

Serves 10

Ingredients:

2½ cups corn, canned or fresh
2 tablespoons butter, melted
2 tablespoons all-purpose flour
1 tablespoon sugar
1 teaspoon salt
⅙ teaspoon pepper
2 eggs
1 cup milk

Directions:

1. Preheat oven to 350°F.
2. Mix corn and butter in large bowl.
3. Add dry ingredients and mix thoroughly.
4. Stir eggs into corn mixture, then add milk and mix well.
5. Pour into greased 9 × 13-inch pan and bake for 30 minutes or until inserted fork comes out clean.

GRANDMA'S OHIO FILLING

Who said filling (or what some call "stuffing") is just for Thanksgiving Day? For the Amish table, filling is a simple side dish served throughout the year with mashed potatoes, gravy, and meat.

Serves 12

Ingredients:

1 loaf white bread, cubed
½ cup butter
2 large potatoes, cut into small cubes
4 carrots, diced
4 stalks celery, chopped
1 cup milk
1 cup chicken broth
2 cups chicken, cooked and chopped
1 teaspoon parsley
1½ teaspoon salt
1 teaspoon pepper

Directions:

1. In large frying pan, toast bread cubes with butter, stirring often until cubes are toasted and brown. Set aside.
2. Preheat oven to 350°F.
3. Boil vegetables until tender, drain, and set aside.
4. In large baking pan, combine toasted bread cubes and cooked vegetables.
5. Add the rest of ingredients and mix well, then bake for 1½ hours, stirring every 30 minutes.
6. Remove from oven and serve.

POTLUCK POTATOES

Even Amish country girls dread picking potato bugs off long rows of plants, but they will laugh at the visiting city boy who doesn't know what to do with his dirty hands on potato digging night. This recipe was a rare treat because of the added ingredients we couldn't grow in our vast garden alongside the humble potato.

Serves 10

Ingredients:

10 potatoes, cubed
1 onion, chopped
1 teaspoon salt
1 (10.5-ounce) can cream of mushroom soup
¼ teaspoon pepper
1½ cups cheddar cheese
1 teaspoon seasoned salt
1 teaspoon parsley flakes
⅛ teaspoon thyme
2 cups sour cream
2 cups cornflakes, crushed

Directions:

1. Preheat oven to 350°F.
2. Boil potatoes, onion, and salt until potatoes are tender. Drain and pour into large baking dish.
3. Add all the rest of the ingredients except cornflakes and stir until mixed.
4. Bake for 30 minutes or until hot and bubbly.
5. Spread crushed cornflakes on top and return to oven for 5 minutes.
6. Remove from oven and serve immediately.

MAKE-AHEAD POTATOES

Whether we're gathered around our own table or another's, hospitality is a big deal in an Amish home. This dish can be made ahead of time and placed in the refrigerator overnight to make for an easier hosting day. It's perfect served alongside baked chicken or meatloaf.

Serves 8

Ingredients:

8 medium potatoes, peeled and boiled
1½ cups sour cream
2 eggs
4 ounces cream cheese
1 teaspoon salt
¼ teaspoon pepper
¼ cup butter
2 cups shredded cheddar cheese

Directions:

1. Cut boiled potatoes in ½-inch cubes. Set aside.
2. Preheat oven to 350°F.
3. In mixing bowl, mix all other ingredients except cheddar cheese. Stir into potatoes and mix.
4. Pour into 9 × 13-inch baking dish.
5. Sprinkle cheese on top and bake for 40 minutes or until hot and cheese is melted.

GRANDMA'S OVEN-FRIED CHICKEN

The chickens we raised at our farm tasted different than store-bought chicken—and Mom knew how to turn the meat into delectably tender and flavorful pieces. Butchering day was long and messy, but we got to enjoy trays of oven-fried chicken all year long.

Serves 8

Ingredients:

1 cup all-purpose flour
1 teaspoon garlic powder
1 teaspoon chicken soup base
1 teaspoon paprika
4 pounds chicken thighs or drumsticks
1 cup water

Directions:

1. Preheat oven to 300°F.
2. Mix flour and seasonings. Coat chicken pieces well. Put water in baking dish. Place chicken in baking dish and bake for 2 hours, then increase oven temperature to 375°F and bake another ½ hour.
3. During the last hour, baste every 15 minutes with liquid from the bottom of the baking dish. If there's not enough liquid to baste, add a bit more water.

CARROT LOAF

I remember pulling long rows of carrots from loose soil until there was an entire wheelbarrow load. Then we'd find a cool place to store them so they could be enjoyed through the long winter months. Or we'd peel and chop enough to fill fifty quart jars, water bathe each jar, and carry the jars to the basement to line dark shelves with orange color. "Carrots make your eyes bright," we were told—and we obediently ate them, year after year.

Serves 10

Ingredients:

1 medium-size onion, chopped
½ cup celery, minced
3 cups carrots, cooked and mashed
2 tablespoons butter
1 teaspoon salt
1½ cups breadcrumbs
1 cup milk
2 eggs, beaten

Directions:

1. Preheat oven to 350°F.
2. Sauté onion and celery in butter, then add to mashed carrots.
3. Stir in all remaining ingredients and pour into 2 bread pans.
4. Bake for 40 minutes.

EASY TACO SKILLET

This dish is perfect for quick dinners after a long day. Make in one large saucepan, serve in the same dish, and spoon out platefuls to your family around the table. This is perfectly paired with Molly's Bread (page 12) and freshly churned butter.

Serves 8

Ingredients:

2 pounds ground beef
1 quart tomato juice
1 ½ cups water
2 tablespoons taco seasoning
¼ cup brown sugar
2 cups white rice, uncooked
2 cups cheddar cheese, shredded
2 cups lettuce, shredded
1 onion, chopped
Sour cream, to taste
Salsa, to taste (page 107)

Directions:

1. Fry beef until browned, then add juice, water, taco seasoning, sugar, and rice.
2. Simmer 20 minutes or until rice is soft.
3. Top with cheese and serve with shredded lettuce, onion, sour cream, and salsa.

FRESH SALSA

Most of these ingredients can be found in the garden where plants are loaded with more tomatoes and peppers than we know what to do with. Various peppers add color and flavor both to garden and dish. Serve this beautiful, nutritious condiment with Amish Haystack (page 128), or any dish you desire!

Makes 1½–2 cups

Ingredients:

1 tomato, large, chopped
1 onion, small, chopped
1 Hungarian wax pepper, chopped
½ green pepper, chopped
1 jalapeño, chopped
½ clove garlic, minced
½ teaspoon honey
1 tablespoon vinegar
⅛ teaspoon pepper
½ teaspoon cumin
½ teaspoon oregano
⅛ teaspoon salt
½ teaspoon lime juice
1 teaspoon fresh cilantro, chopped
1 teaspoon fresh parsley, chopped

Directions:

1. Mix vegetables and spices thoroughly, then store in a glass jar in refrigerator.

DANDELION EGG "A LA MODE"

With three well-rounded meals served each day, Mom had to get creative. We loved this egg gravy served for lunch or dinner. Feeding chickens and gathering eggs in bare feet was a normal childhood task and sometimes, if I waited long enough, I got to see an egg roll out from beneath a chicken. And we loved running outside to gather dandelion greens for the gravy.

Serves 6

Ingredients:

¼ cup butter
¼ cup all-purpose flour
2 cups milk
Salt and pepper, to taste
4 hard-boiled eggs
Dandelion greens
Whole wheat toast with butter

Directions:

1. Melt butter in saucepan and stir in flour.
2. Slowly pour in the milk, stirring constantly with whisk. Heat and stir until boiling, then toss in greens. Season with salt and pepper.
3. Slice hard-boiled eggs and gently stir into sauce.
4. Serve over buttered toast.

MOM'S BUTTERNUT SQUASH CASSEROLE

Each fall, Mom took us kids out to the garden where we'd harvest butternut squash into a wheelbarrow and store them upstairs in a cool, dark closet to enjoy for the next months. Most times, she'd cook them in chunks and serve with butter, salt, and pepper. We loved it all, but this casserole was special.

Serves 8

Ingredients:

4 cups cooked and mashed butternut squash
2 eggs, beaten
⅔ cup milk
⅔ cup butter, room temperature, divided
½ teaspoon salt
¾ cup brown sugar
½ cup all-purpose flour
1½ teaspoons cinnamon
1 cup chopped walnuts

Directions:

1. Preheat oven to 350°F.
2. Divide fresh butternut squash in half and bake for 1 hour or until soft. Leave oven on.
3. Remove seeds and mash until smooth.
4. Add beaten eggs, milk, ⅓ cup butter, and salt.
5. Mix well and pour into 9 × 13-inch baking dish.
6. Mix brown sugar, flour, cinnamon, walnuts, and remaining ⅓ cup butter until crumbly. You can use your fingers for this.
7. Sprinkle evenly on top of casserole and bake for 30 minutes.

BROCCOLI CASSEROLE

Mom took great joy in growing her broccoli plants for as long as possible in the summer months. From soups to casseroles, we knew it was good for us to eat, and we weren't allowed to pass it by or complain!

Serves 8

Ingredients:

10 cups broccoli florets, chopped
1 cup shredded cheddar cheese
1 (10.5-ounce) can cream of mushroom or celery soup
2 eggs
1 cup mayonnaise
2 tablespoons chopped onion
2 packages Ritz crackers, crumbled
2 tablespoons melted butter

Directions:

1. Preheat oven to 350°F.
2. Boil broccoli until tender. Drain and set aside.
3. Mix cheese, soup, eggs, mayonnaise, and onion, then carefully mix into broccoli.
4. Place into a 9 × 13-inch baking dish.
5. Mix melted butter and crumbled crackers together, then spread evenly over broccoli.
6. Bake for 45 minutes or until browned and bubbly.

MAKE-AHEAD BEEF ENCHILADAS

We were always excited when Mom brought this delicious casserole to the table. Spicy sauce, cheddar cheese, and ground beef makes this a welcome and hearty variation to any table. If you have any left over, it'll be just as delicious reheated the next day!

Serves 10

Ingredients:

1½ pounds lean ground beef
1 onion, chopped
1 green pepper, chopped
3¾ cups shredded cheddar cheese, divided
1 (4-ounce) can chopped green chilies
1 (15-ounce) can black beans, rinsed and drained
¾ tablespoon dried minced garlic
¾ tablespoon chili powder
⅓ tablespoon paprika
¾ tablespoon cumin
2 teaspoons salt
½ teaspoon black pepper
1 (28-ounce) can enchilada sauce
10 burrito-style flour tortillas

Directions:

1. In a large frying pan, brown ground beef with the onions and peppers. Add green chilies, black beans, and all the seasonings.
2. Preheat oven to 350°F.
3. Place about ⅓ cup filling and ⅛ cup shredded cheddar on a tortilla. Fold 1 side, tuck 2 ends in, and roll to form enchilada. Place in 9 × 13-inch baking pan. Repeat until filling is used up.
4. Cover generously with sauce and top with remaining cheese and dried cilantro.
5. Bake, uncovered, for 30 minutes.

YUMMASETI

My Aunt Sheryl used to make this dish when both our families got together. Whether it was butchering day or play day, we always had fun and there was plenty of food for the many cousins running around the farm. This dish is easy to prepare and makes feeding a crowd appear simple!

Serves 10

Ingredients:

1 pound noodles (any kind)
1 (10.5-ounce) can cream of mushroom soup
2 cups frozen peas
1 (10.5-ounce) can cream of celery soup
2 pounds ground beef
1 onion, chopped
1 teaspoon salt
½ teaspoon pepper
10 slices Velveeta cheese
4 cups bread, cubed
½ cup butter

Directions:

1. Boil noodles for 8 minutes, then drain and add mushroom soup.
2. Place noodles in bottom of 4-quart casserole dish.
3. Boil peas until tender, drain, and add celery soup. Spread over noodle layer.
4. In a frying pan, brown ground beef with onion, salt, and pepper. Spread over pea layer.
5. Cover with Velveeta cheese.
6. Preheat oven to 350°F.
7. Melt butter in frying pan, then add bread cubes and stir as they toast. Sprinkle with additional salt and pepper, toasting until golden brown.
8. Spread bread cubes on top of casserole and bake for 30 minutes.

MOM'S GROUND TURKEY CASSEROLE

An easy, one-dish casserole making good use of the humble potato, this dish sparks flavor with black pepper and onion. Mom layered it early and baked it slowly, then served it with applesauce and homemade bread with butter. We loved it!

Serves 10

Ingredients:

2 pounds ground turkey
1 teaspoon salt
1 teaspoon black pepper to taste
¼ teaspoon cayenne pepper
1 onion
3–4 cups green beans, cut into 1-inch pieces
5–6 cups potatoes, peeled and sliced thin

Directions:

1. Preheat oven to 350°F.
2. In a frying pan, brown ground turkey with seasonings. Put into a 4-quart casserole dish.
3. Thinly slice onion and arrange slices on top of ground turkey.
4. Spread green beans on top of onion layer.
5. Add half the potato slices, sprinkle with salt, and add remaining potatoes.
6. Sprinkle with salt and pepper.
7. Bake for 60 minutes or until vegetables are soft.

SAUSAGE RICE CASSEROLE

This casserole is nourishing and delicious, with spicy sausage slices bringing flare to rice seasoned with pizza flavor and mozzarella cheese. We thought it a welcome, spicy diversion from the usual meat and potatoes menu!

Serves 10

Ingredients:

5 cups cooked rice
2 pounds Polish kielbasa, sliced
1 (15-ounce) can diced tomatoes
2 zucchinis, sliced
1 onion, diced
2 green peppers, diced
2 tablespoons pizza seasoning
Salt and pepper to taste
3–4 cups shredded mozzarella

Directions:

1. Preheat oven to 350°F.
2. Spread rice into 9 × 13-inch cake pan.
3. In large pan, sauté all vegetables and sausage. Add seasoning, salt, and pepper to taste.
4. Spread mixture over rice, top with cheese, and bake until heated and cheese is melted.

MOM'S BARBECUE MEATBALLS

It took a lot of meatballs to feed a family of twelve, so these were an extra treat at the table, accompanied by potatoes of some kind, a vegetable, and of course bread and butter. You can't have any Amish meal without a large loaf of bread and butter!

Serves 12

Ingredients:

Meatballs:

3 pounds ground beef
1 ⅓ cups milk
2 cups quick oats
1 cup onion, chopped
¾ teaspoon salt
¾ teaspoon pepper
¾ teaspoon garlic powder

Sauce:

2 cups ketchup
1 ½ cups brown sugar
⅛ teaspoon liquid smoke

Directions:

1. Preheat oven to 350°F.
2. Combine meatball ingredients well, then form into 1¼-inch balls and place on a cookie sheet.
3. Bake for 30 minutes.
4. Combine sauce ingredients, then spread over meatballs and bake 15 minutes longer.

CHICKEN AND DUMPLINGS

Mom put these dumplings over her chicken stew, but you could serve these soft and tasty biscuits with any soup or stew. Your family will love these!

Serves 10

Ingredients:

3 cups all-purpose flour
1 teaspoon salt
6 teaspoons baking powder
2 eggs, beaten
4–6 tablespoons milk
Filling from Chicken Pot Pie recipe (page 79)

Directions:

1. Combine dry ingredients, then add beaten eggs and milk. Stir just until mixed.
2. Prepare the filling from Mom's Chicken Pot Pie recipe. Leave in large kettle, then drop teaspoons of dumpling dough over bubbling stew.
3. Simmer slowly on very low heat for 10 minutes or until dumplings no longer appear sticky on top.
4. Place kettle in center of table and ladle into bowls immediately.

AUNT LINDA'S BAKED MACARONI AND CHEESE

Everyone knows Aunt Linda is a real foodie, and her Amish dishes are the best. After eating this dish, you'll never again lift a box of mac 'n' cheese off the grocery shelf. Two cheeses in a sauce made from scratch accent every bite of pasta beautifully!

Serves 10

Ingredients:

7 tablespoons butter, divided
3 tablespoons all-purpose flour
2 cups milk
2 cups shredded cheddar cheese
½ cup white American cheese, sliced
½ teaspoon salt
¼ teaspoon pepper
2 cups macaroni pasta, cooked and drained
¾ cup bread cubes

Directions:

1. Preheat oven to 350°F.
2. Melt 4 tablespoons butter in saucepan, then slowly stir in flour. Add milk, stirring constantly with wire whisk over low heat until thick and bubbly. Add salt and pepper.
3. Add cheese to milk and stir until all cheese is melted.
4. Place cooked pasta in 9 × 13-inch pan, then pour cheese sauce over top.
5. In a frying pan, brown bread cubes in remaining 3 tablespoons of butter, then spread over top of casserole and bake, uncovered, for 1 hour.

AMISH HAYSTACK

This versatile dish was a favorite as I was growing up. We love the crunch of Ritz crackers or tortilla chips, and the fact that most anything layered on top brings happy smiles to the family table.

Serves 6

Ingredients:

3 cups rice, cooked
1 pound ground beef
¾ tablespoon taco seasoning
¼ teaspoon salt
Tortilla chips or Ritz crackers
2 cups lettuce, shredded
1 tomato, diced
1 onion, diced
1 cup shredded cheddar cheese

Cheese Sauce:

1 pound American cheese slices
1 ⅓ cups water
⅛ teaspoon baking soda
⅛ teaspoon salt

Directions:

1. In a frying pan, brown the ground beef with taco seasoning and salt.
2. Put remaining ingredients in separate serving bowls.
3. To make the cheese sauce, place the American cheese in a small saucepan then add water, baking soda, and salt. Melt on medium heat, stirring frequently. Once the cheese has fully dissolved and no lumps remain, remove from heat and allow to cool.
4. Layer the elements in whatever order you wish and enjoy!

Cookies and Whoopie Pies

Baker's Secret

GINGER ROLLED COOKIES

There's nothing like a soft ginger cookie, but these are extra special with cut-out designs and a glossy egg shine to the top. If you have children, this is your edible playdough moment with results everyone in the family will enjoy!

Makes 80 cookies

Ingredients:

½ pound brown sugar
1 cup lard
2 cups buttermilk
2 cups molasses
1 tablespoon baking soda
1 tablespoon ginger
½ teaspoon salt
½ teaspoon alum or cream of tartar
4½ cups all-purpose flour
1 egg, beaten

Directions:

1. Mix sugar, lard, buttermilk, and molasses together in large mixing bowl. Add dry ingredients and mix thoroughly.
2. Chill overnight.
3. Preheat oven to 350°F. Roll dough out to ¼-inch thick, dusting both dough and counter with a sprinkling of flour to prevent sticking.
4. Cut into desired shapes, and place on cookie sheet.
5. Brush with beaten egg and bake for 10 minutes or until light brown and still soft to the touch. Over-baking will result in a crunchy cookie, and we like these soft and chewy.
6. Store in a covered container at room temperature.

AUNT BENA'S CHOCOLATE COOKIES

Seeing these dark brown cookies sandwiched with wh te frosting on my grandmother's table is one of my fondest childhood memories. There were far too many desserts to sample and my stomach would fill quickly, especially because we'd already been served multiple meat and potato dishes. But the platters of cakes and pies paled in my young eyes in comparison to these fun chocolate shapes oozing with creamy white frosting.

Makes 40 sandwich cookies

Ingredients:

Cookies:

2 cups brown sugar
½ cup butter
3 eggs
¼ cup cocoa powder
4 cups all-purpose flour
1 teaspoon vanilla
1 teaspoon baking soda

Frosting:

2 egg whites
1 teaspoon vanilla
4 cups powdered sugar, divided
1½ cups Crisco

Recipe Note: The egg whites in this recipe are not cooked, but you could substitute them with liquid pasteurized egg whites to be safer. Consuming raw egg whites may pose a risk of foodborne illness, including salmonella infection. Individuals with weakened immune systems, pregnant women, young children, and older adults should avoid raw eggs unless pasteurized.

Directions:

1. Mix brown sugar, butter, and eggs until mixture is smooth and creamy.
2. Add dry ingredients and mix thoroughly.
3. Chill for a few hours or until firm to the touch.
4. Preheat oven to 350°F. Roll dough to desired thickness, using extra flour on counter to prevent sticking.
5. Cut into shapes and bake for 10 minutes or until set but soft to the touch.
6. Cool to room temperature.
7. Meanwhile, make the frosting. Beat egg whites until stiff, add vanilla and 2 cups powdered sugar. Mix thoroughly, then add remaining 2 cups powdered sugar and Crisco. Whip together until smooth and fluffy.
8. When cookies are cool, sandwich with frosting and store in a covered container at room temperature.

GRANDPA WEAVER'S SUGAR COOKIES

Plain sugar cookies were a staple for our family. Sometimes Mom dusted each cookie in powdered sugar before placing them in a five-gallon bucket for us to grab when we were hungry from running around on the farm or working in the garden. Special sugar cookie days meant coating the tops with frosting and decorating them with raisins. This recipe makes a lot of cookies. If you're not baking for a crowd, freeze some cookies for another time!

Makes 100 cookies

Ingredients:

5 eggs
½ cup lard
½ cup butter
½ cup sour cream
3 cups brown sugar
½ teaspoon baking soda
2 teaspoons baking powder
5½ cups all-purpose flour

Directions:

1. Preheat oven to 350°F. Grease a baking sheet.
2. Mix ingredients in order given, adding baking soda, baking powder, and flour last.
3. Drop by teaspoonful onto greased baking sheet and bake for 10 minutes or until very light brown.
4. Remove to rack and cool until room temperature.

PEANUT BUTTER FINGERS

With ten children in the home, there wasn't money for store-bought treats, but we often had homemade goodies. These cookie bars were like candy bars to us, and we made them often. Pouring glaze on top while they're still hot from the oven allows everything to settle in soft, chewy layers.

Makes 16 bars

Ingredients:

1 cup butter
2 cups brown sugar
⅔ cup peanut butter
2 eggs
½ teaspoon salt
1 teaspoon baking soda
1 teaspoon vanilla
2 cups oatmeal
2 cups all-purpose flour

Glaze:

3 tablespoons water
2 tablespoons butter
¼ cup cocoa powder
1 cup powdered sugar
½ teaspoon vanilla

Directions:

1. To make the cookie layer, preheat oven to 350°F. Mix butter and sugar together until creamy. Add peanut butter and eggs, then stir briskly until blended.
2. Add remaining ingredients and stir well.
3. Grease the bottom of a 9 × 13-inch pan, then spread dough evenly into pan.
4. Bake for 30 minutes or until browned and lightly set. In the meantime, mix up the glaze.
5. Place water and butter in saucepan and bring to a boil.
6. Add cocoa powder and blend with whisk.
7. Add powdered sugar and vanilla and blend well.
8. Remove bars from oven and immediately cover with chocolate glaze. Cool and cut into squares. Store covered at room temperature.

CUTOUT SUGAR COOKIES

An Amish child's first happy memory often includes a sugar cookie. These are similar to my Grandpa Weaver's sugar cookies, with more of a solid texture which makes them perfect to decorate or sandwich with various colored frostings.

Makes 60 cookies

Ingredients:

1¼ cups sugar
1¼ cups butter
2 eggs
¾ tablespoon vanilla
¾ teaspoon baking soda
¾ teaspoon salt
3¼ cups all-purpose flour

Directions:

1. Use a hand or stand mixer to blend sugar, butter, eggs, and vanilla thoroughly.
2. Add dry ingredients and mix well.
3. Cool overnight or a few hours until dough is stiff to the touch.
4. Preheat oven to 350°F. Roll out dough and cut into desired shapes, using flour on counter to prevent sticking.
5. Bake for 10–12 minutes or until light brown. Remove to a rack to cool.
6. Store in a covered container and enjoy for many days!

MONSTER COOKIES

With peanut butter and chocolate pairing in a chewy cookie with crunchy edges, these are hard to pass by. When my oldest sister grew up and moved to Africa, Mom's monster cookies were on top of her list of things missed. Seven sisters, now with homes of our own, and we all agree this recipe must be handed down through the generations!

Makes about 140 cookies

Ingredients:

1 cup butter, softened
2 cups brown sugar
2 cups white sugar
2 cups smooth peanut butter
6 eggs
2 teaspoons vanilla
4 teaspoons baking soda
1 teaspoon salt
1 tablespoon corn syrup
9 cups old-fashioned oats
2⅓ cups mini chocolate chips
2⅓ cups M&Ms

Directions:

1. Preheat oven to 350°F. Grease a cookie sheet or line with parchment paper.
2. In a large bowl, cream together butter, brown sugar, and white sugar.
3. Mix in the peanut butter, eggs, and vanilla until combined.
4. Add baking soda, salt, and corn syrup and mix.
5. Stir in the oats and then the chocolate chips and M&Ms.
6. Use a 2-tablespoon cookie scoop to scoop dough onto prepared cookie sheet, leaving about 1 inch between each cookie. Press dough down slightly.
7. Bake for 10–15 minutes or until they look just set. Allow to cool on the pan before removing to a rack.
8. Store in a covered container at room temperature. These cookies can also be frozen and enjoyed later!

CHOCOLATE WHOOPIE PIES

Whoopie pies are the most well-known Amish cookie. Considered a vital part of the pantry, these take more time and are a bit more special than the common sugar cookie. But patience is a virtue in the Amish woman's kitchen, and she spends many hours there daily. Whoopie pies are just one of the items she bakes without second thought!

Makes 40 filled whoopie pies

Ingredients:

Cookies:

2 cups white sugar
1 cup butter
2 eggs
2 teaspoons vanilla
4½ cups all-purpose flour
2 teaspoons baking soda
½ teaspoon salt
1 cup cocoa powder
1 cup water
1 cup milk

Frosting:

2 egg whites
1 teaspoon vanilla
4 cups powdered sugar, divided
1½ cups Crisco

Recipe Note: Consuming raw egg whites may pose a risk of foodborne illness, including salmonella infection. Substitute with liquid pasteurized egg whites to be safer. Individuals with weakened immune systems, pregnant women, young children, and older adults should avoid raw eggs unless pasteurized.

Directions:

1. To make the cookies, preheat oven to 350°F.
2. Blend sugar, butter, eggs, and vanilla in large mixing bowl. Set aside.
3. In another bowl, mix flour, baking soda, salt, and cocoa powder. Set aside.
4. Mix water and milk, then add dry mixture to sugar mixture in small amounts along with small amounts of liquid. Repeat until everything is combined. (Dough will be runnier than most cookie dough.)
5. Drop by teaspoonful on ungreased cookie sheet about 2 inches apart and bake for 7 minutes or until cookie is set and slightly firm to the touch.
6. Cool until room temperature.
7. Meanwhile, make the frosting. Beat egg whites until stiff, then add vanilla and 2 cups powdered sugar. Mix thoroughly, then add remaining 2 cups powdered sugar and Crisco. Whip together until smooth and fluffy.
8. Spread a cookie with a generous amount of frosting and sandwich another cookie on top. Repeat with remaining cookies.

UNCLE ABNER'S PUMPKIN WHOOPIE PIES

Pumpkin makes a delightful variation of the famous Amish whoopie pie. Moist and soft, you will love the pumpkin flavor and cake-like texture bursting with cream cheese frosting (or filling, as the Amish call it). This is a year-round favorite but even more special in the fall!

Makes 40 filled whoopie pies

Ingredients:

3 cups brown sugar
1 cup vegetable or canola oil
2 cups pumpkin puree
2 eggs
1 teaspoon vanilla
3 cups all-purpose flour
1 teaspoon salt
1 teaspoon baking soda
1 teaspoon baking powder
1 teaspoon cinnamon
1 batch Cream Cheese Frosting (page 169)

Directions:

1. Preheat oven to 350°F.
2. With a hand or stand mixer, blend sugar, oil, pumpkin, and eggs thoroughly. Add vanilla and mix.
3. Add dry ingredients and mix well.
4. Drop by teaspoonful on ungreased cookie sheet about 2 inches apart.
5. Bake for 10–12 minutes or until set and slightly firm to the touch.
6. Cool and sandwich with cream cheese frosting.
7. Store in a covered container in a single layer or layered with parchment paper to prevent sticking.

FRUIT-TOPPED COOKIES

These cookies are shared to remember my brother Peter, who passed away some years ago and left us with memories of him smiling behind an entire counter of these deliciously soft, fruity cookies. A cake-like sugar cookie paired with fruit filling unites cookie and pie in the best of culinary worlds. Peter agreed.

Makes 80 cookies

Ingredients:

2 cups brown sugar
1 cup butter
2 eggs
1 tablespoon vanilla
4 tablespoons milk
1 teaspoon baking soda
4 cups all-purpose flour
Pie filling of choice

Directions:

1. Preheat oven to 350°F.
2. Using a hand or stand mixer, blend sugar, butter, eggs, vanilla, and milk.
3. Add baking soda and flour and mix well. If needed, add a small amount of additional flour to create a dough stiff enough to form into walnut-sized balls.
4. Place balls of cookie dough onto ungreased baking sheet, then dip your thumb into cold water and create an indentation halfway into the cookie. Keep shaping the hole about ¼ inch to the edges, creating a round hole.
5. Fill the hole with your choice of pie filling.
6. Bake for 10 minutes or until lightly browned.
7. Cool and store in a cool area, covered and layered with parchment paper to prevent sticking.

Cakes and Cupcakes

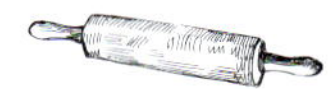

MOM'S REDAWIKE CUPCAKES

Biting into these soft chocolate cream-filled cupcakes is one of my favorite childhood memories. Sometimes, Mom added peanut butter to half of her frosting for two different flavors and colors. We loved both!

Makes 24 cupcakes

Ingredients:

Cupcakes

¾ cup vegetable oil
2 cups sugar
3 eggs
1 teaspoon vanilla
2¼ cups all-purpose flour
2 teaspoons baking soda
2 teaspoons baking powder
¾ cup cocoa powder
1 cup milk
1 cup brewed coffee

Mom's Buttercream Frosting

1 cup butter, softened
4½ cups powdered sugar
1 teaspoon vanilla
2–4 tablespoons cream or water

Directions:

1. Preheat oven to 350°F and line a cupcake tray.
2. Mix oil and sugar, then add eggs and vanilla, beating well.
3. Mix dry ingredients in a separate bowl.
4. Stir wet and dry mixtures together alternately with milk.
5. Lastly, add coffee and mix well.
6. Fill each cupcake liner ⅔ full and bake for 20 minutes or until cupcake is firm to touch.
7. Remove from oven and cool.
8. Meanwhile, make the frosting. Place softened butter in mixing bowl. Add 1 cup powdered sugar and beat well, scraping sides of bowl to ensure no lumps are left.
9. Add vanilla and remaining sugar along with 2 tablespoons cream or water. Mix thoroughly for 5 minutes, adding more liquid slowly if needed to create a smooth and spreadable frosting. If you get it too thin by accident, simply add more powdered sugar and keep mixing until you have what you desire.
10. Now you can assemble the cupcakes. With a sharp knife, cut a hole about 1-inch in diameter out of the top center of each cupcake and save the cut piece.
11. Mound each hole generously with Mom's Buttercream Frosting, then place cut piece on top of frosting for a color-contrasted look.

MOM'S BUTTERSCOTCH CAKE

Mom's basic yellow cake rose to a soft, spongy texture before she covered it with her buttercream frosting or whipped cream and strawberries. Sometimes this was a regular oblong cake and other times it was a layered round cake smothered in homemade vanilla pudding and chocolate glaze. Whatever the case, we hope you have as much fun with this delectable basic as we do!

Serves 20

Ingredients:

4 eggs
2 cups sugar
2 cups all-purpose flour
2 teaspoons baking powder
¼ teaspoon salt
1 cup milk
2 tablespoons butter
1 teaspoon vanilla

Directions:

1. Preheat oven to 350°F.
2. Beat eggs until light and fluffy.
3. Add sugar and beat again for 5–10 minutes. The mixture should be light and almost frothy.
4. Add dry ingredients.
5. In a saucepan, heat milk and butter to boiling, then add to above mixture, mixing well.
6. Add vanilla and mix.
7. Pour into 9 × 13-inch cake pan and bake for 30 minutes or until inserted toothpick comes out clean.
8. Remove from oven and cool before covering with your favorite frosting.

BOSTON CREAM CAKE

When guests arrived, Mom often layered her basic yellow cake with homemade vanilla pudding and chocolate glaze to create a tall, beautiful dessert. A creamy center and glossy topping complement a soft, sponge-like cake perfectly!

Serves 12

Ingredients:

1 recipe batter from Mom's Butterscotch Cake (page 154)
1 recipe pudding from Banana Creme Pie recipe (page 182)
2 cups chocolate chips
1 cup half-and-half

Directions:

1. Preheat oven to 350°F.
2. Make batter for Mom's Butterscotch Cake.
3. Grease 2 (9-inch) round cake pans and line with parchment paper, then evenly divide cake batter between pans.
4. Bake for 30 minutes or until toothpick inserted in center comes out clean.
5. Let cool completely, then remove from pans.
6. Make pudding from Banana Creme Pie recipe.
7. Let cool.
8. Place 1 round cake on platter, then load up with cooled pudding, then place the other cake on top.
9. Melt chocolate chips with half-and-half, then pour over top of cake and let drizzle down the sides.
10. Store in refrigerator and serve chilled.

APPLE BUTTER LAYER CAKE

This cake is soft and moist with true apple flavor and warm spices. We loved harvesting free apples by the roadside or in a friend's yard as it was a versatile fruit that lasted for months in storage. If you love apples, you will love this cake!

Serves 16

Ingredients:

¾ cup butter
1¼ cups sugar
3 eggs
½ cup milk
1½ cups apple butter
3 cups all-purpose flour
1½ teaspoons baking soda
¾ teaspoon salt
¾ teaspoon nutmeg
¾ teaspoon cinnamon
¾ teaspoon cloves
Mom's Buttercream Frosting (page 154)

Directions:

1. Preheat oven to 350°F. Grease 2 (8-inch) round cake pans.
2. Mix butter, sugar, eggs, milk, and apple butter until smooth.
3. Add dry ingredients and stir until well blended.
4. Pour into cake pans and bake for 30 minutes or until toothpick inserted in center comes out clean.
5. Cool, then remove from pans and layer with frosting.
6. Store in refrigerator and enjoy for days as this cake is better with age!

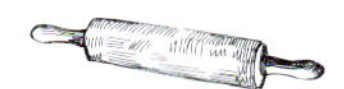

RHUBARB UPSIDE-DOWN CAKE

Mom's rhubarb plants were massive edible bouquets of crunchy goodness that we'd cut at the base and then lick and try to endure the sour flavor shocking our taste buds. We thought it much better chopped, soaked in sugar, and baked under a soft oatmeal cake. Our cake didn't need ice cream beside it on the plate—a simple cup of milk from the cow was perfect!

Serves 16

Ingredients

⅔ cup water
½ cup rolled oats
2 tablespoons butter, melted
1 cup white sugar, divided
2½ cups chopped rhubarb
1 cup all-purpose flour
1 teaspoon baking powder
¼ teaspoon baking soda
¼ teaspoon salt
½ teaspoon cinnamon
½ cup brown sugar
¼ cup oil
1 egg

Directions:

1. Boil water and pour over oats. Set aside to soak for 20 minutes.
2. Preheat oven to 350°F.
3. Mix melted butter and ⅓ cup white sugar. Sprinkle rhubarb over sugar-butter mixture and set aside.
4. Stir together flour, baking powder, baking soda, salt, and cinnamon, then set aside.
5. In another bowl, mix ⅔ cup white sugar and brown sugar, oil, and egg.
6. Add oatmeal mixture and mix thoroughly.
7. Add flour mixture and mix well.
8. Place rhubarb mixture in 9 × 13-inch pan and carefully pour cake batter over it, then bake for 30 minutes or until toothpick inserted in center comes out clean. If desired, invert cake onto platter before serving.

PINEAPPLE UPSIDE-DOWN CAKE

We love this cake served warm after a hearty meal. Crispy cake edges merge with brown sugar topping alongside bursts of pineapple over a soft, sponge-like yellow cake reminding the palate of butterscotch and caramel. Truly decadent!

Serves 16

Ingredients:

4 eggs
2 cups white sugar
2 cups all-purpose flour
2 teaspoons baking powder
¼ teaspoon salt
1 cup milk
½ cup plus 2 tablespoons butter
1 teaspoon vanilla
1 cup brown sugar
1 (20-ounce) can pineapple rings, drained

Directions:

1. Preheat oven to 350°F.
2. Beat eggs until light and fluffy.
3. Add white sugar and beat again for 5–10 minutes. The mixture should be light and almost frothy.
4. Add flour, baking powder, and salt.
5. Heat milk and 2 tablespoons butter to boiling, then add to above mixture, mixing well.
6. Add vanilla and stir.
7. In 9 × 13-inch pan, melt ½ cup butter and spread evenly over pan. Sprinkle 1 cup brown sugar over top. Place pineapple rings over sugar.
8. Pour cake batter slowly over pineapple rings and bake for 40–50 minutes or until toothpick in center comes out clean.
9. Remove from heat and allow to cool about 10 minutes (no longer). Take a knife around edges of pan to dislodge cake, then flip onto a tray, upside down.
10. Serve warm or cold.

MOM'S FAMOUS CARROT CAKE

Mom's carrot cake travels with her when she visits us in other states. We place multiple forks in the pan and dig right in, making communal carrot cake our new tradition. Pineapple gives a tropical flare to each bite, while cream cheese frosting oozes from the layers. And everyone knows I recommend a double recipe of the frosting!

Serves 12

Ingredients:

Cake:

2 cups all-purpose flour
2 teaspoons baking powder
1 ¼ teaspoons baking soda
1 teaspoon salt
¾ teaspoon cinnamon
4 large eggs
2 cups white sugar
2 teaspoons vanilla extract
1 ¼ cups vegetable oil
2 cups shredded carrots
1 (20-ounce) can crushed pineapple
1 cup shredded coconut

Cream Cheese Frosting:

20 ounces cream cheese, room temperature
8 tablespoons butter, room temperature
1 teaspoon vanilla extract
¼ teaspoon salt
4½ cups powdered sugar

Topping:

1 cup sweetened coconut flakes, toasted

Directions:

1. Preheat oven to 350°F.
2. Butter 3 (8-inch) round cake pans, then line the bottoms with parchment paper.
3. In medium-sized bowl, whisk together flour, baking powder, baking soda, salt, and cinnamon. Set aside.
4. In another bowl, beat eggs, sugar, and vanilla until light and frothy. Add oil and beat well.
5. Mix in flour mixture, just until blended.
6. Fold in carrots, pineapple, and coconut, then divide batter evenly in between pans and bake for 30 minutes or until toothpick inserted in center comes out clean.
7. Remove from oven and let cool for 15 minutes, then remove cake from pans and finish cooling.
8. Meanwhile, make the frosting. In a medium-sized bowl, beat cream cheese, butter, and vanilla until smooth. Add salt and powdered sugar and beat until smooth and creamy.
9. Frost cake, then sprinkle with toasted coconut flakes.

MOM'S OATMEAL CAKE

Large pots of oatmeal were common breakfast food, but when Mom turned oatmeal into a cake with brown sugar topping, we thought oats reached a new level. Inexpensive and easy to prepare, this cake was one of the few Mom could afford to make more frequently even when grocery money was tight for feeding ten children. Frugality created plenty, and there were always leftovers on the table.

Serves 16

Ingredients:

Cake:

1¼ cups boiling water
1¼ cups quick oatmeal
½ cup butter
1 cup brown sugar
1 cup white sugar
2 eggs
1½ cups all-purpose flour
1 teaspoon baking soda
1 teaspoon nutmeg, optional
1 teaspoon cinnamon
½ teaspoon salt
1 teaspoon vanilla

Topping:

6 tablespoons butter
¼ cup heavy cream
⅔ cup brown sugar
1 teaspoon vanilla
1 cup coconut
1 cup chopped walnuts

Directions:

1. Pour boiling water over oats and set aside for 20 minutes.
2. Preheat oven to 350°F.
3. Mix butter and sugars well, then add eggs one at a time, beating well each time.
4. Mix in oat mixture.
5. Sift flour, baking soda, spices, and salt, then add to batter.
6. Add vanilla, mix, then pour into greased 9 × 13-inch cake pan. Bake for 30–35 minutes.
7. To make the topping, melt butter with cream and brown sugar. Simmer for 30 minutes, then remove from heat and add the vanilla, coconut, and walnuts. Pour over cake as soon as it comes out of the oven.
8. Enjoy hot or cold!

CREAM CHEESE FROSTING

We love this versatile frosting on a variety of things, but a special treat is cinnamon rolls with cream cheese frosting. From carrot cake to oatmeal sandwich cookies, you can't go wrong enhancing baked goods with this recipe!

Makes about 3½ cups frosting, enough for a 2-layer cake

Ingredients:

8 ounces cream cheese
4 tablespoons softened butter
2 teaspoons vanilla
1 pound powdered sugar
1 tablespoon milk, if needed

Directions:

1. Beat cream cheese and butter until smooth, then add vanilla and sugar, a few cups at time, beating well each time.
2. Carefully add a tablespoon of milk if frosting is too stiff, then mix again until desired thickness.

Pies, Pastries, Puddings, and Ice Cream

PENNSYLVANIA DUTCH SHOOFLY PIE

If you peek into an Amish pantry, you'll see shoofly pies on the shelves, waiting to be enjoyed—sometimes twice daily. Grandma often woke at 4:00 in the morning to bake her shoofly pies, then took a nap when the bulk of her chores were finished. She served breakfast after her early baking, and of course shoofly pies were included!

Makes 4 pies

Ingredients:

4 bottom piecrusts (page 185)

Liquid Mixture:

⅔ cup brown sugar
8 eggs
3 cups shoofly molasses or Golden Barrel Table Syrup
3 cups water, boiling
2 teaspoons baking soda

Dry Mixture:

6 cups all-purpose flour
2 cups brown sugar
1 teaspoon baking soda
½ teaspoon salt
¼ teaspoon cream of tartar
1½ cups butter

Directions:

1. Line 4 pie plates with bottom pie crusts.
2. Preheat oven to 425°F.
3. To make the liquid mixture, mix brown sugar and eggs with a whisk, then add molasses.
4. Mix boiling water and baking soda, then add to egg mixture and set aside.
5. For dry mixture, mix flour, brown sugar, baking soda, salt, and cream of tartar. Cut in butter until crumbly.
6. Add 4 cups dry mixture to liquid mixture, then distribute evenly into 4 piecrusts.
7. Sprinkle remaining dry mixture on top.
8. Bake for 10 minutes, then lower oven heat to 350°F for another 40–50 minutes or until inserted toothpick comes out clean.

GRANDMA'S COCONUT OATMEAL PIE

This pie is a more economical version of the classic pecan pie, but no less tasty. With a crunchy surface, cake-like center, and gooey bottom, each bite is bursting with both texture and flavor. A true Amish classic!

Makes 4 pies

Ingredients:

3 cups brown sugar
1½ cups butter
3 cups light molasses
8 eggs, well beaten
½ teaspoon baking soda
1 cup water
1 cup coconut
3 cups quick oats
1 cup walnuts
4 bottom piecrusts

Directions:

1. Preheat oven to 350°F.
2. Mix all ingredients (except piecrusts) in order given, then distribute evenly into 4 unbaked piecrusts.
3. Bake for 40 minutes or until center is browned and firmly set.

GRANDMA WEAVER'S APPLE PIE

Peeling fresh apples at lightning speed is a skill Amish girls learn simply by watching their mothers. While Dad loved seeing how long he could get the peel to curl beyond his knife before it broke and fell, Mom zipped her knife around apple after apple, trying to get enough peeled and sliced to get four pies in the oven before it was time to start making dinner.

Makes 2 pies

Ingredients:

2 double piecrusts (page 185)
1 cup brown sugar
¼ cup all-purpose flour
¼ teaspoon salt
¾ cup water
1 tablespoon vanilla
2 tablespoons butter
9 cups apples, peeled and thinly sliced

Directions:

1. Preheat oven to 350°F.
2. Line 2 pie plates with bottom piecrusts.
3. In saucepan, mix sugar, flour, and salt.
4. Add water, vanilla, and butter. Bring to a boil and simmer until thick and creamy.
5. Pour over apple slices and mix, then distribute evenly into 2 piecrusts.
6. Cover with top piecrusts and bake for 45 minutes or until crusts are light brown.
7. Serve warm or cold with vanilla ice cream.

STRAWBERRY ICE CREAM PIE

This version of strawberry pie always brought a smile to the family table. We think the chewy, crispy rice crust topped with ice cream and red berries makes this pie one to remember and make often! For other variations of this pie, fill with any ice cream and topping of choice. You can't go wrong!

Makes 1 pie

Ingredients:

4 cups vanilla ice cream
4 cups crispy rice cereal
½ cup smooth peanut butter
½ cup corn syrup
3 cups strawberries, sliced

Directions:

1. Take ice cream out of freezer and allow to soften.
2. Mix cereal, peanut butter, and corn syrup together, then press into pie pan, rounding edges on the rim.
3. Fill with softened ice cream.
4. Slice fresh strawberries on top and serve immediately.

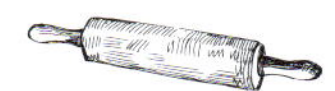

DARLENE'S APPLE PIE

In an Amish kitchen, pies are a staple and usually served immediately after the main course. Apples are easily purchased or harvested, and you may see a horse and carriage beside the road, waiting as a mom and her kids pick up free apples that would otherwise be wasted.

Makes 4 pies

Ingredients:

4 double piecrusts (page 185)
18 cups diced or thinly sliced apples
1 ½ cups sugar
1 tablespoon cinnamon
2 tablespoons all-purpose flour
½ teaspoon salt
½ cup butter
½ cup cream or half-and-half

Directions:

1. Preheat oven to 350°F.
2. Line 2 pie plates with bottom piecrusts.
3. Place apple slices in large mixing bowl, then add the rest of the ingredients except butter and cream and mix well.
4. Distribute evenly into piecrusts.
5. Divide stick of butter into 4 equal parts, then slice on top of apples in piecrusts.
6. Drizzle cream over apples.
7. Cover with top crusts and bake for 45 minutes or until tops are lightly browned.

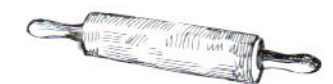

MOM'S BANANA CREME PIE

I loved making this pie for my parents and nine siblings. One pie was never enough, so this recipe was often quadrupled. The pies would last a mere few days, but the effort was always worth seeing the joy on faces around the family table. I do believe this pie gave us the energy needed to run the farm and family business! Start this recipe the day before serving so the pies have time to chill.

Makes 1 pie

Ingredients:

½ cup sugar
3 tablespoons cornstarch
⅛ teaspoon salt
2 eggs
2 cups milk
1 tablespoon butter
1½ teaspoons vanilla, divided
1 cup heavy whipping cream
½ cup powdered sugar
1 bottom piecrust (page 185)
2 ripe bananas

Recipe Notes: For Peanut Butter Creme Pie, mix 1½ cups powdered sugar and ½ cup peanut butter until crumbly. Spread half of mixture into baked piecrust, fill with pudding, top with whipped cream, and sprinkle remaining crumbs on top.

For Coconut Creme Pie, place ¾ cups coconut into baked piecrust, fill with pudding, top with whipped cream, and sprinkle another ¾ cup coconut on top.

Directions:

1. Mix sugar, cornstarch, and salt, then add eggs and stir until smooth. Set aside.
2. Heat milk, watching carefully until it's almost to boiling.
3. Lower heat and slowly stir in sugar mixture, stirring constantly as it returns to a bubbly simmer.
4. When pudding is thick, remove from heat and add butter and 1 teaspoon vanilla.
5. Immediately pour into a baked piecrust, let set, and cool.
6. Refrigerate until the next day, then whip cream until very thick and add ½ teaspoon vanilla and powdered sugar.
7. Slice one banana directly on top of pudding, cover pie with a thick layer of whipped cream, then slice another banana on top.
8. Serve immediately.

1/4
CUP

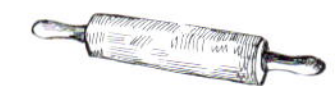

MOM'S PIECRUST

I spent so much time watching Mom make piecrusts that she barely had to teach me before I was rolling, crimping, and filling multiple pie crusts in one baking session. This recipe can be used for any piecrust recipe in this book or elsewhere. From Chicken Pot Pie to Coconut Creme Pie, look no further!

Makes top and bottom crust for 2 pies

Ingredients:

5 cups all-purpose flour
2 teaspoons baking powder
½ teaspoon salt
2 cups lard or shortening (like Crisco)
1 egg
1 tablespoon white vinegar
1 cup water

Directions:

1. In large mixing bowl, mix flour, baking powder, and salt before adding lard or shortening, mixing with your hands until mixture is crumbly.
2. Beat egg and add vinegar, then add water and stir.
3. Slowly drizzle water mixture into flour mixture, stirring with your hand as you go.
4. When all crumbs stick together, stop adding water and press dough into a firm ball. Do not knead—the less mixing, the better!
5. Dust a countertop with flour to prevent sticking, then divide dough into 4 even portions.
6. Roll out 2 portions of dough ⅛-inch thick. Sprinkle flour as needed to prevent sticking, then place gently into 2 pie pans.
7. Fill with pie filling of choice.
8. Roll out remaining 2 portions of dough and cut slits in dough for steam escape. Moisten edges of crust lightly with water, then place top crust onto pie and press firmly around edges to prevent pie filling from seeping out.
9. Crimp around edges and bake as instructed in each pie recipe.

Recipe Notes: For an already baked piecrust, use this recipe and place in pie pan, then take a fork to poke holes all over piecrust, including the sides.

Bake at 350°F for 15–20 minutes or until crust is light brown.

Cool and fill with your favorite cream pie filling.

Makes 4 bottom piecrusts.

MOM'S PUMPKIN CUSTARD PIE

My brother could eat half of one of these custard-like pumpkin pies in one sitting. Mom left them sitting on the countertop or in the pantry for him to grab whenever he wanted during his busy work days. He'd grab a slice, hold it in his hands, and devour it in seconds. For our family of twelve, four of these pies lasted perhaps two days.

Makes 4 pies

Ingredients:

4 bottom piecrusts (page 185)
4 cups pureed pumpkin
2 cups brown sugar
2 cups white sugar
6 tablespoons all-purpose flour
2 teaspoons salt
1 teaspoon nutmeg
1 teaspoon cinnamon
3 cups milk
3 cups heavy cream
6 eggs, separated

Directions:

1. Preheat oven to 350°F.
2. Line 4 pie plates with piecrusts.
3. Mix all remaining ingredients in order given, adding egg yolks last while reserving egg whites.
4. Whip egg whites until stiff and peaked.
5. Gently fold egg whites into pumpkin mixture, just until mixed.
6. Pour into 4 piecrusts and bake for 60 minutes or until center is firm.
7. Remove from oven and cool. Store in refrigerator.

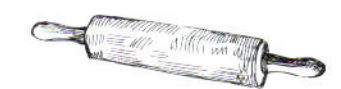

LEMON PIE

On an Amish table, various pies are a common sight after main course and often eaten on the same plates as the first course. Children are required to finish food and expected to eat what is served without complaint, and then they get to enjoy some of the best desserts there are. Lemon pie was a less common pie in our home, but a welcome treat!

Makes 1 pie

Ingredients:

3 tablespoons cornstarch
1 ¼ cups plus 6 tablespoons sugar, divided
1 tablespoon grated lemon rind
3 eggs, separated
¾ cup lemon juice
1 ½ cups boiling water
1 piecrust (page 185), baked and cooled

Directions:

1. Combine cornstarch, 1¼ cups sugar, and lemon rind.
2. Beat egg yolks and lemon juice and add to cornstarch mixture.
3. Gradually add boiling water, then heat to boiling again, stirring constantly until thick.
4. Remove from heat and pour into piecrust refrigerate until cool.
5. Beat egg whites until stiff, then add remaining 6 tablespoons sugar.
6. Top cooled pie with egg whites and return to refrigerator until serving.

Recipe Note: Consuming raw egg whites may pose a risk of foodborne illness, including salmonella infection. Substitute with liquid pasteurized egg whites to be safer, though you may need to whip them for longer and they may not reach the same volume as fresh egg whites. Individuals with weakened immune systems, pregnant women, young children, and older adults should avoid raw eggs unless pasteurized.

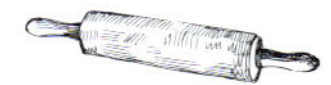

JANTZI'S APPLE CRUMB PIE

I love an apple crumb pie enough to double the topping ingredients. You can never have too much crunchy, yet soft, topping on warm baked apples resting in a flaky crust. Fresh apples and ordinary flour combine to make this pie magical on all accounts. Serve warm with vanilla ice cream!

Makes 1 pie

Ingredients:

1 unbaked bottom piecrust (page 185)

Filling:

2 cups apples, sliced thinly
¾ cup white sugar
¼ teaspoon salt
3 tablespoons all-purpose flour
1 egg
½ teaspoon vanilla
1 cup sour cream

Crumb Topping:

⅓ cup brown sugar
1 teaspoon cinnamon
½ cup all-purpose flour
⅓ cup butter

Directions:

1. Preheat oven to 350°F.
2. Line pie plate with piecrust.
3. Mix all filling ingredients thoroughly and pour into unbaked piecrust.
4. Combine crumb topping ingredients and spread over filling.
5. Bake for 45 minutes or until browned and bubbly.

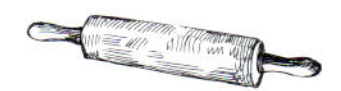

VANILLA PUDDING

Some Amish kids love this pudding served warm, with saltine crackers crumbled into the bowl. We loved it any way and every way, hot or cold—and with extra milk from the cow to use up, Mom made this often. Instead of purchasing ice cream from the store, Amish moms often serve this vanilla pudding with cake.

Serves 5

Ingredients:

1 quart plus 2 tablespoons milk, divided
¾ cup sugar
1 heaping tablespoon cornstarch
⅛ teaspoon salt
2 eggs
1 tablespoon vanilla
2 tablespoons butter

Directions:

1. Put 1 quart milk in saucepan and set aside.
2. Mix sugar, cornstarch, salt, eggs, and additional 2 tablespoons milk with whisk, until smooth.
3. Heat milk to almost boiling point, watching carefully.
4. Slowly whisk in sugar mixture, stirring constantly.
5. Simmer slowly as you stir, until pudding is thick and creamy.
6. Remove from heat and add vanilla and butter.
7. Cool, stirring periodically with whisk, then store in refrigerator.

AUNT SADIE'S CARAMEL SAUCE

The Aunties arrived at our house for visits with their own bunch of children and huge boxes of cookies or desserts. The only problem was not having enough room in our stomachs for all the wonderful food they cooked all day as we ran wild and set up our own make-believe kitchens out of sticks and grass.

Makes 2½–3 cups

Ingredients:

1½ cups sugar
½ cup butter
1 teaspoon baking soda
¾ cup buttermilk (or create your own by adding 1 teaspoon white vinegar to ¾ cup milk)
2 tablespoons honey
2 teaspoons vanilla

Directions:

1. Combine all ingredients except vanilla in saucepan and bring to boil, stirring constantly. Simmer 5 minutes.
2. Remove from heat and add vanilla.
3. Cool and store in glass jar, refrigerated.
4. Serve over cake or ice cream.

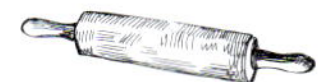

MOM'S FRUIT CRISP

Dessert was served most days at our house, and this was an easy one made hundreds of times for our household. From fresh apples to canned cherry pie filling, the variations to this delicious favorite has no limits. Amish kids often pour milk over this dessert, but topped with ice cream is an extra treat.

Serves 10

Ingredients:

3 cups quick oats
1 ½ cups brown sugar
1 ½ cups all-purpose flour
¼ teaspoon baking soda
¼ teaspoon baking powder
1 ⅓ cups butter, room temperature
Favorite fruit pie filling

Directions:

1. Preheat oven to 350°F.
2. Mix oats, sugar, flour, baking soda, and baking powder in large bowl, then cut in butter until crumbly.
3. Sprinkle crumbs evenly on top of your favorite fruit pie filling and bake for 30 minutes.
4. Serve warm or cold.

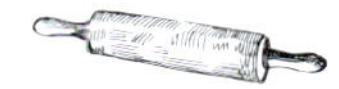

PUMPKIN ROLL

This roll may look complicated to create, but it's relatively simple after the first time. I like to double the filling—my family knows I think it useless to create this dessert unless the filling is as thick as the cake. No bite should ever wonder where the cream cheese is!

Serves 8

Ingredients:

Pumpkin Roll:

3 eggs
⅔ cup pumpkin puree
1 cup sugar
¾ cup all-purpose flour
1 teaspoon cinnamon
1 teaspoon soda

Filling:

1 (8-ounce) package cream cheese
¼ cup butter, softened
1 cup powdered sugar, plus more for dusting
1 teaspoon vanilla

Directions:

1. Start with the pumpkin roll: Preheat oven to 350°F. Mix eggs, pumpkin, and sugar together, beating well until smooth.
2. Add dry ingredients and mix well.
3. Grease and layer a 10 × 12-inch cookie sheet with parchment paper, then spread pumpkin mixture evenly over paper.
4. Bake for 12 minutes, keeping a careful eye on it to give or take a few minutes. You want to remove it from heat as soon as it's set firmly.
5. While pumpkin roll is baking, sprinkle a kitchen towel liberally with powdered sugar and leave on counter. When you remove the pumpkin roll from the oven, immediately turn the cookie sheet over and allow the pumpkin roll to fall onto the towel.
6. Lift the cookie sheet off, remove the parchment paper, then start at one end and roll the towel up with the pumpkin roll inside. Leave it rolled up and cool completely.
7. To make the filling, mix cream cheese, butter, powdered sugar, and vanilla well.
8. When pumpkin roll is cooled, unroll carefully, leaving towel underneath.
9. Spread evenly with cream cheese filling, then roll back up without towel and carefully lift onto an oblong platter.
10. Sprinkle top with powdered sugar.
11. Refrigerate or slice and serve immediately!

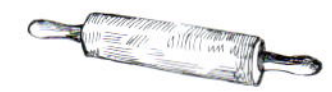

FRUIT COBBLER

Freshly made whipped cream tops this cobbler off beautifully. You can use any cherry or berry as a base under this cake-like topping—or, as Amish often do, simply pour milk over your bowl of cobbler.

Serves 10

Ingredients:

1 ½ cups all-purpose flour
½ cup sugar
1 ½ teaspoons baking powder
½ teaspoon salt
3 tablespoons butter
½ cup milk
8–10 cups fruit pie filling

Directions:

1. Preheat oven to 350°F.
2. Mix dry ingredients first, then crumble in butter, and lastly, add milk.
3. Stir just until moistened.
4. Place rounded teaspoons of dough over top a 9 × 13-inch cake pan of your favorite pie filling.
5. Bake for 20–30 minutes until fruit filling is bubbling and hot and cobbler mounds are light brown. Do not over-bake!

NO-BAKE CHERRY CHEESECAKE

Desserts like this one, with all the store-bought ingredients, were a rare treat in our home growing up. Fast and easy, this can be thrown together in a matter of minutes while bringing a whole lot of joy to your table.

Serves 8

Ingredients:

2 (8-ounce) blocks cream cheese
¾ cup white sugar
1 teaspoon vanilla
1 container Cool Whip
1 graham cracker pie crust
1 (12-ounce) can cherry pie filling

Directions:

1. Blend cream cheese, sugar, and vanilla. Fold in Cool Whip and spread into piecrust.
2. Top with cherry pie filling and chill 2 hours before serving.

CREAMY HOMEMADE ICE CREAM

Growing up, our cow often produced more milk than we needed, and we never wanted it to go to waste. The thick cream that formed at the top could be churned into butter or delicious, creamy ice cream. Dad taught us how to add the correct amounts of ice and salt into the wooden case surrounding the ice cream churn, and we used all our young arm power to turn that handle until the mixture turned thick.

Serves 12

Ingredients:

2 tablespoons unflavored gelatin
½ cup cold water
1 ⅓ cups sugar
1 teaspoon salt
1 cup cocoa powder, optional
4 cups whole milk, divided
3 cups heavy cream
2 tablespoons vanilla

Directions:

1. In a small bowl, add gelatin to cold water. Mix and let set until jelled and thick.
2. In large saucepan, mix sugar, salt, and cocoa powder (if you want chocolate ice cream). Slowly stir in 2 cups milk.
3. Heat on medium heat, stirring constantly until sugar is dissolved and milk scalded (hot but not boiling).
4. Remove from heat, whisk in gelatin, then stir in remaining milk, cream, and vanilla.
5. Pour into 4-quart ice-cream freezer and churn until thick.
6. Enjoy with any of your favorite desserts!

AMISH DATE PUDDING

You won't get much better than a solid date cake layered with thick whipped cream and caramel in a large glass bowl. Fit for your daily family table or holiday meals, this dessert will add beauty and flair to any occasion—and we think caramel sauce the perfect addition to these beautiful layers!

Serves 10

Ingredients:

1 cup chopped dates
1 tablespoon butter
2 cups boiling water
1 cup sugar
2 eggs, beaten
2½ teaspoons vanilla extract, divided
3 cups all-purpose flour
2 teaspoons baking soda
Pinch salt
1 cup chopped walnuts
1 pint whipping cream
3 heaping tablespoons powdered sugar
1 (4-ounce) jar caramel sauce

Directions:

1. Preheat oven to 350°F.
2. Put chopped dates into a large bowl. Add butter and pour boiling water over the top. Let set for about 5 minutes, stirring occasionally.
3. Add sugar, beaten eggs, and 2 teaspoons vanilla. Mix well.
4. Add flour, baking soda, and salt. Mix.
5. Stir in the chopped nuts.
6. Pour into a well-greased 9 × 13-inch cake pan. Bake for 25–30 minutes or until a toothpick comes out clean.
7. Cool and cut into 1-inch squares.
8. Whip cream until thick, then add powdered sugar and remaining ½ teaspoon vanilla.
9. Layer cake squares, whipped cream, and caramel sauce in large glass bowl, repeating layers until ingredients are used.
10. Store overnight and serve the next day.

Canning, Cheese, and Miscellaneous

MOZZARELLA CHEESE

Our Jersey cow constantly supplied more milk than we needed—so, we learned how to make cheese. Stretchy and white, this cheese is fun to snack on or add to your favorite casseroles. You can shred it, slice it, or break it off in chunks for your kids to snack on. And, it is surprisingly easy to make!

Serves 12

Ingredients:

5 teaspoons citric acid powder
1 gallon water plus 1 cup cold water, divided
4 gallons fresh milk
¼ rennet tablet
1½ cups salt

Directions:

1. Dissolve citric acid powder into ½ cup cold water, then stir into milk.
2. In large kettle, heat milk mixture to 98°F.
3. Dissolve rennet tablet in ½ cup cold water and add to milk mixture. Let set undisturbed and covered for ½ hour.
4. Cut into 1-inch squares and let set 15 minutes until whey separates. Heat to 110°F, stirring often to keep curds from forming or sticking.
5. Remove from heat and stir occasionally for another 20 minutes, then drain in colander for 15 minutes.
6. Meanwhile, heat 1 gallon water with 1½ cups salt to 170°F.
7. Pull cheese apart with your hands, place in bowl, pour heated water over it and begin stretching it with wooden spoons in an upward motion. It will stretch into long, smooth strings of cheese. Keep stretching it for 5 minutes, then place in bread pans and allow to cool.
8. Refrigerate, then slice or break off in chunks to enjoy with fresh bread and soup.

FANNIE'S VANILLA YOGURT

Anyone with a food thermometer can make this recipe! I made countless containers of this yogurt for my parents and siblings, often topping it with homemade granola or canned peaches. Simple, easy, inexpensive, and delicious—yogurt truly can be made in the kitchen at home!

Serves 16

Ingredients:

1 gallon milk
2 tablespoons plain gelatin
½ cup cold water
1 cup plain yogurt
1 cup sugar
2 tablespoons vanilla

Directions:

1. Heat milk to 190°F.
2. Meanwhile, soak gelatin in ½ cup cold water, then add to milk when it reaches 190°F.
3. Let cool until it reaches 130°F.
4. Stir yogurt, sugar, and vanilla into milk until dissolved.
5. Pour into containers, then wrap containers in a big bath towel and let set overnight or at least 8 hours or until yogurt is firm.
6. Store in refrigerator in an airtight container for up to 2 weeks.

HOME-CHURNED BUTTER

Our Jersey cow always gave us heavy cream that rose to the top of each gallon of milk. We skimmed this off carefully to keep it thick and condensed enough for butter. Making butter is simple yet difficult on the arms if you don't have a butter churn, but it can be done and is a fun project for children. This was a family chore in the old farmhouse and we all got stronger because of it. There's nothing like golden fresh butter on homemade bread straight out of the oven!

Makes 4 cups

Ingredients:

2 quarts heavy cream
1 teaspoon salt

Directions:

1. Pour cream into glass gallon jar and shake vigorously until butter lumps are obvious. This will take a while and it helps to have a hand-turned butter churn, but it's not a must.
2. When butter lumps are obvious, take a slotted spoon (I grew up using my hands) to pull butter together and into a bowl.
3. When all butter lumps are in bowl, squeeze them into a ball, then wash butter with cold water, kneading butter until water runs clear and no more butter milk appears.
4. Add salt and shape into ball, then place on a platter and enjoy!

AMISH PEANUT BUTTER

Considered a staple in Amish homes, bowls of this peanut butter grace tables at weddings and funerals as well as every family table. Thick slices of soft homemade bread are smothered in this—and now that I'm older, it tastes more like dessert, though Amish kids think this a side dish to enjoy with any regular meal.

Makes 13–14 cups

Ingredients:

2½ cups brown sugar
2 cups white sugar
2 cups water
⅔ cup molasses
2½ pounds peanut butter
1 pint marshmallow crème

Directions:

1. Mix sugars, water, and molasses in saucepan and boil for 2 minutes.
2. Cool, then add peanut butter and marshmallow crème. Stir well and store in covered jar or container.
3. Serve with homemade bread and enjoy!

CANNED DILL PICKLES

Mom loved canning pickles, so we spent hours in the garden harvesting small cucumbers from prickly vines. Not our favorite chore, but we loved the crispy results and ate many quart jars full throughout the winter. Mom mastered the art of creating the perfect crispy pickle by timing the minutes in the cold pack process just right—and you'll never find a dill pickle off a grocery store shelf with the same flavor!

Makes 2 quarts

Ingredients:

Fresh cucumbers, sliced
1 head fresh dill
½ teaspoon minced garlic, fresh or jarred
2 tablespoons salt
4 cups water
2 cups vinegar
¼ teaspoon turmeric

Directions:

1. Fill canning jars to the neck ring with sliced cucumbers, then place a head of fresh dill and ½ teaspoon garlic on top.
2. Heat all other ingredients in large saucepan, then pour into jars, again to the neck ring.
3. Place covered jars in canner and fill with water to the neck ring of the jars. Bring to a boil.
4. Cold pack (boil) for 10 minutes, then remove jars from water, tighten rings, and let seal and cool on countertop.

Recipe Note: Mom always placed a large towel on her countertop to catch extra water and protect the counter! Use whatever amount of cucumbers you have, and simply make more of the dill juice if necessary. Amish women don't measure everything because they never know how much will come out of the garden on a given day!

PICKLED RED BEETS

An Amish table knows pickled red beets like it knows bread and butter. Both sweet and sour, this side dish adds unique flavor to the basic meat and potatoes and is considered a necessity on the basement shelves before summer is over. Personally, I love red beets cooked and served as a vegetable even more—and I'll never forget the nutritious, flavorful taste of the humble red beet out of the family garden!

Makes 2 pints

Ingredients:

Fresh red beets
1 cup vinegar
2 cups sugar
1 tablespoon salt
⅛ teaspoon pepper
2 cups red beet water

Directions:

1. Wash however many beets you have from your garden and place them, whole, in a large saucepan. Cover with water and boil until beets are soft.
2. Remove cooked beets from water, then cool, peel, and slice beets before filling canning jars to the neck ring with sliced beets.
3. Save 2 cups of the water beets were cooked in, then add all other ingredients and cook just until heated.
4. Pour beet juice mixture into jars up to the neck ring.
5. Cover and place jars in large canner, fill with water up to the neck ring, and cold pack (boil) for 10–15 minutes.
6. Remove jars from hot water, tighten lids, and let seal and cool on countertop.

HOMEMADE APPLE BUTTER

A perfect fall day is the house full of bubbling apple butter smells and Mom musing over it until the thick brown mixture is perfectly baked. Spread over scrapple for breakfast or homemade bread for lunch, this apple butter is the perfect combination of apples, cinnamon, and brown sugar!

Makes 8–9 pints

Ingredients:

16 cups plain applesauce
6 cups brown sugar
1 cup apple cider vinegar
2 tablespoons cinnamon

Directions:

1. Preheat oven to 350°F.
2. Combine all ingredients and bake in large roast pan (the kind you cook your Thanksgiving turkey in) for 3–4 hours, stirring every hour or so.
3. Fill jars up to neck ring, cover, and place in canner.
4. Fill canner with water up to neck ring of jars and cold pack (boil) for 10–15 minutes.
5. Remove jars from canner, tighten lids, and let seal and cool on countertop.
6. Serve with *everything!*

GRANDMA LAPP'S OYSTER CRACKERS

Grandma's pantry always had two things in them—seasoned oyster crackers and shoofly pie. She'd pull out large containers of this salty snack and we thought it the best thing ever! Dill weed and ranch dressing flavor the oil coating for a savory, salty treat. These crackers can be stored in the pantry for weeks.

Makes 18–22 cups

Ingredients:

1 bag pretzels
1 ¼ cups canola oil
¾ teaspoon garlic salt
1 teaspoon dill weed
1 teaspoon celery salt
1 package dry ranch dressing mix
1 (24-ounce) bag oyster crackers

Directions:

1. Mix everything except crackers in a large bowl. Add crackers and stir until each piece is coated.
2. Stir occasionally over the next few hours, then store in an airtight container and enjoy for weeks!
3. Optional: For crispier crackers, spread on a cookie sheet and bake at 350°F for 30 minutes.

LAUNDRY SOAP

A five-gallon bucket of this soap makes laundry economical for large families. One may not realize these simple ingredients can be found in your local Walmart laundry isle. Keep safely out of reach from toddlers as this recipe makes a five-gallon bucket of liquid.

Makes 4 gallons

Ingredients

⅔ bar Fels-Naptha, grated
1 cup washing soda
1 cup Borax
Water

Directions:

1. In large saucepan, melt Fels-Naptha in 12 cups water.
2. Add washing soda and Borax; stir until melted.
3. Pour 8 cups water into 5-gallon bucket, add soap mixture, and stir until mixed.
4. Add 2¾ gallons water and stir.
5. Store, covered, at room temperature.
6. Use 1 cup per load of laundry.
7. Keep safely out of reach of all toddlers and young children.

METRIC CONVERSIONS

If you're accustomed to using metric measurements, use these handy charts to convert the imperial measurements used in this book.

Weight (Dry Ingredients)

1 oz		30 g
4 oz	¼ lb	120 g
8 oz	½ lb	240 g
12 oz	¾ lb	360 g
16 oz	1 lb	480 g
32 oz	2 lb	960 g

Oven Temperatures

Fahrenheit	Celsius	Gas Mark
225°	110°	¼
250°	120°	½
275°	140°	1
300°	150°	2
325°	160°	3
350°	180°	4
375°	190°	5
400°	200°	6
425°	220°	7
450°	230°	8

Volume (Liquid Ingredients)

½ tsp.		2 ml
1 tsp.		5 ml
1 Tbsp.	½ fl oz	15 ml
2 Tbsp.	1 fl oz	30 ml
¼ cup	2 fl oz	60 ml
⅓ cup	3 fl oz	80 ml
½ cup	4 fl oz	120 ml
⅔ cup	5 fl oz	160 ml
¾ cup	6 fl oz	180 ml
1 cup	8 fl oz	240 ml
1 pt	16 fl oz	480 ml
1 qt	32 fl oz	960 ml

Length

¼ in	6 mm
½ in	13 mm
¾ in	19 mm
1 in	25 mm
6 in	15 cm
12 in	30 cm

INDEX

D

E

R

S

ALSO AVAILABLE

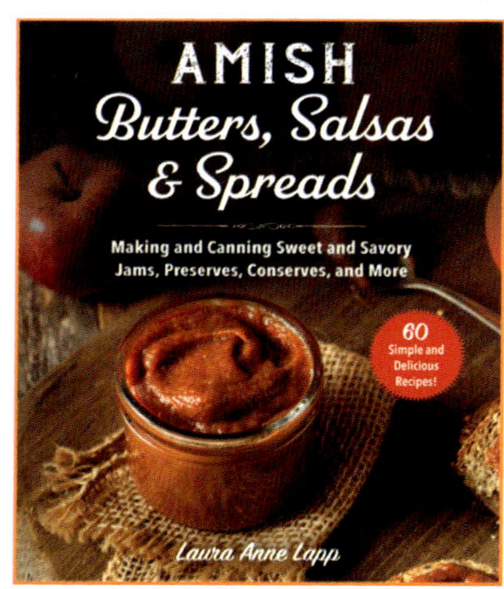

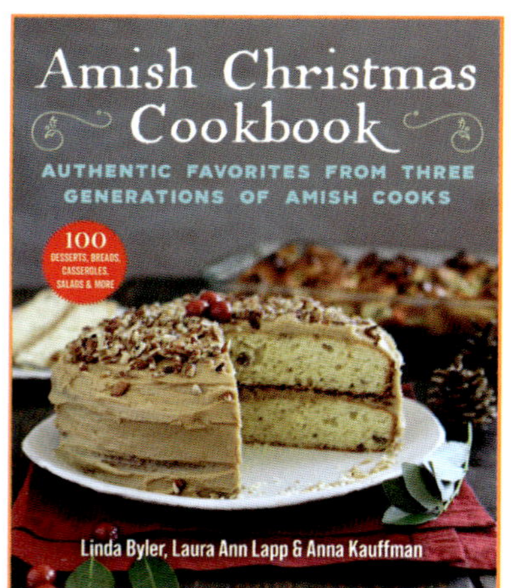

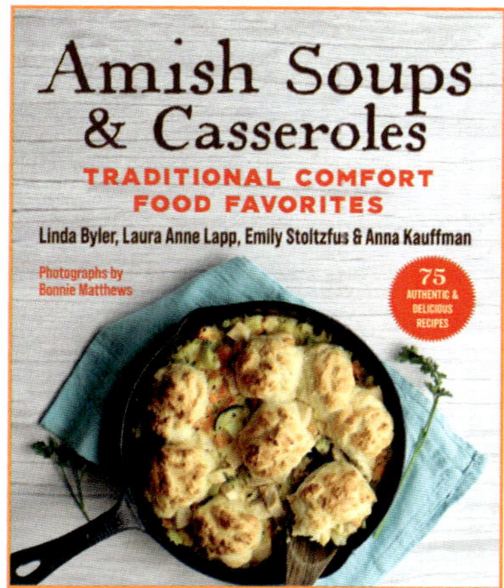